RAB C. NESBITT

The Scripts

RAB C. NESBITT

The Scripts

IAN PATTISON

STARRING *Gregor Fisher as Rab C Nesbitt*

BBC BOOKS

As scribe on this book I should like to thank Colin Gilbert for producing and directing *Rab C. Nesbitt* on television and Nigel Robertson for taking the photographs.

IAN PATTISON, July 1990

Published by BBC Books,
a division of BBC Enterprises Limited,
Woodlands, 80 Wood Lane, London W12 0TT
First published 1990

Cover and inside photographs by Nigel Robertson

ISBN 0 563 36042 9

Set in 10/11½ Janson by Ace Filmsetting Ltd, Frome
Printed and bound in Great Britain by Redwood Press Ltd, Melksham
Cover printed by Richard Clay Ltd, St. Ives plc, England

Contents

Rab C. Nesbitt

As a new man, I support the struggle of women to free themselves from the yoke of male domination.

Rab C. Nesbitt

EPISODE ONE

CAST LIST

RAB C. NESBITT	Gregor Fisher
MAN IN BUS QUEUE	Leon Sinden
BURNEY	Eric Cullen
MARY NESBITT	Elaine C. Smith
GASH	Andrew Fairlie
JAMESIE	Tony Roper
DODIE	Iain McColl
ANDRA	Brian Pettifer
DOUGIE	Charlie Sim
HOSIE	Matthew Costello
DHSS CLERK	Lee Cornes
WOMAN IN QUEUE/PARK ATTENDANT	Dorothy Paul (Stuntwoman: Denise Ryan)
BUS DRIVER	Ray Jeffries
MARY'S MOTHER	Irene Sunters
MARY'S FATHER	Leonard Maguire
MAN IN SUPERMARKET	Russell Hunter

Rab C. Nesbitt

SCENE 1. A bus stop. Morning.
People waiting in a bus queue to go to work. Nesbitt staggers along, a string of sausages dangling from his pocket.

NESBITT. (*To audience.*) What a night, by the way, what a night! It lasted three days. She sent me oot to go get a pound of sausages for the tea, then I meets a wee mate, next thing I know it's Thursday. But that's me, a free spirit, know? (*To man in bus queue.*) You got a lend of a fag there please, pal? (*Man gives him a fag.*) Thanks very much. (*To second person in queue.*) You got a light there, please, Jim? (*Second man gives him a light.*) Cheers. (*To third person.*) You got an ashtray there please, doll? Just kidding! Just kidding! Just a whacky kinna guy, know? Miserable bitch. (*To all.*) Zis youse on your way to work by the way?

They all look at him.

It's awright. I know yeez are shy. I'll do the talking. My God, look at the state of yeez, eh. Zis what work does for yeez, by the way? Is it? If it's that bad, why don't yeez jack it in and join the civil service?

MAN IN QUEUE. That's a cheap remark. I happen to be a civil servant. And I work damn hard for my money. Unlike some!

NESBITT. What'd you mean, what'd you mean? I've got a job, pal. I'm a therapist.

MAN IN QUEUE. A therapist?

NESBITT. (*Holding imaginary willy, aiming.*) Aye, there a piss, there a piss! (*To woman in queue.*) Aye, I see you like the body jokes, eh, hen? Is that why you married him?

WOMAN IN QUEUE. Look, would you please go away and leave us all in peace.

MAN IN QUEUE. Here comes the bus. Thank goodness!

Bus arrives. Passengers get on, off.

NESBITT. (*To audience.*) See, that's another thing about life these days. There's no human contact. I mind the time when total strangers would stop each other in the street, say 'what the hell are you looking at, broken nose?' And there'd maybe be a wee flash of steel, a wee puddle of blood and then offski. Maybe I'm sentimental. But I look back on them days as being kinna like

8

the golden age of criminal violence, know? See nooadays, they don't know what fun is. (*Slaps side of bus, to driver.*) Awright, Boris. Take them to the labour camps! (*Showing clenched fist.*) Work is freedom! Work is freedom!

Bus drives off. Nesbitt shudders.

Tell yeez one thing but.

He steps into the street, raising his hands to halt the traffic. A car screeches to a halt. He carries on, casually talking to camera.

D'you ever get thon feeling that maybes you've pushed your luck a bit too far? And that maybes fate's gonny give you a wee dunt on the napper with the toecap. That's the feeling I've got the noo. (*Reaching into pocket.*) I got her this box of sweeties afore I hit the bucket on Monday there. I'm hoping that them and the old silver tongue'll be enough to do the business for me, know? (*Swallows.*) Need to scrape the fur off it first, mind yi. Tell you one thing about me, boy. I could charm the birds off the trees, by the way, so I could. (*Stops another car.*) Get to . . . ! Gawn . . . !

SCENE 2. The Nesbitt's living room. Day.
Nesbitt enters, singing. We see a pair of women's slippered feet toasting by the fire. Cigarette smoke rising from behind an armchair. A letter stands on the mantlepiece; O.H.M.S.

NESBITT. (*Singing.*) I love you, for sentimental reasons . . . (*Approaching chair from the back.*) Sorry I'm late back, darlin. But there was a helluva queue in Prestos. (*Proffering.*) Here a wee somethin' to say how much I care.

Burney, in the chair, takes the sweets.

BURNEY. Thanks very much, da. I've a bit of a crush on you mysel . . .

NESBITT. (*Hitting him with sweets.*) Shuttit you! Where's your mother?

BURNEY. Aya!

NESBITT. Where's your mother?

BURNEY. She's in the bedroom, packing her suitcase.

NESBITT. Her suitcase. What for?

Mary enters.

9

Yes, the revolutionary new Govan
diet can lose you sixteen stone of unsightly fat. Just keep feeding
the tube this muck and he'll be deid by Christmas.

MARY. Burney son, have you seen my slip . . . (*She clocks Nesbitt, but speaks to Burney.*) Is that him back?

BURNEY. I don't know, Maw. (*To Nesbitt.*) Is that you back, Da?

NESBITT. (*Hitting him.*) Shuttit you!

BURNEY. Aye, blame me. It's aye the weans that suffer in a marital break up.

He fires an air pistol at an unframed picture of Nesbitt, tacked to the wall.

NESBITT. What marital break up? Mary, darling. Is there something wrang? Do I detect unpleasantness here?

Mary flings some stuff into a holdall.

MARY. You're bliddy right you do, pal! I've had my fill of you, Rab Nesbitt. You make me sick, with your drunken carrying on, and your low-life pals! You're totally irresponsible! (*Indicating*

10

Burney.) See that wean there, that wean's got more responsibility in his wee finger than you've got in your entire body!

BURNEY. You said it, Maw. (*Wriggling it.*) And that's not even my trigger finger. (*He takes another potshot.*)

MARY. (*Slapping him.*) Cut that out!

Gash enters from the bedroom.

GASH. Hey, gonny youse keep the rammy doon! I'm trying to winch a lassie in there!

BURNEY. (*To Gash.*) Hey, plookface. You want to take a good dekko at this. This'll be youse in a few years time.

Gash takes a look at the two hatchet faces.

GASH. (*Calling into bedroom.*) Hey, bitch! Get your coat on, you're leaving!

He exits.

NESBITT. So is that it then? You're saying you're going. After all we've been through the gither.

MARY. It's *because* of all we've been through that I'm going. For Christ's sake, open your eyes. Look at this place. Look at the way we're living.

Gash enters with his girlfriend.

GASH. That's me away, Maw.

MARY. I widnae bring a dog back to a place like this!

BURNEY. (*To Gash.*) You wid, widn't yi. (*To girlfriend.*) Yi should see some of the hounds he's had by the way, doll.

GASH. (*Showing fist.*) Shuttit you! Wait to I get you. (*To Mary.*) Hey Maw.

MARY. What is it?

GASH. Just a casual enquiry, Maw. I just want to know if youse are going to be separated when I get back.

MARY. I don't know. How?

She sits, lights a fag, agitated.

11

GASH. Coz if yeez are, I'll bring back chips that's all. I don't much fancy my Da's cooking.

NESBITT. Less of that talk you! I'll have no talk of separation in my hoose!

BURNEY. Gonny get me a bag as well. I'll give you the dosh.

GASH. (*Going.*) Right . . .

NESBITT. What is this! What is this! Am I hearing right here? After all I've done for yeez! (*Shouting at Mary.*) After all the love I've splattered on yi, all these years, you're giving me the hipsway! Is that it?

MARY. Don't try that stuff with me, Rab Nesbitt. I sent you oot for a punna sausages three days ago, and I still never seen hide nor hair of them.

NESBITT. Sausages? Sausages? What're you talking ab . . . (*Sniffs.*) Oh aye. (*Reaching into pocket.*) I wondered what that funny smell was. (*Proffering.*) Here's your sausages.

MARY. (*Knocking them away.*) I don't want them noo! They're no good to me noo!

NESBITT. Och Mary, Mary look at me. You and I go back a long way. We've known each other too long to let a punna deid meat come between us.

MARY. Let's leave wur sex life out of this. I'm talking about wur relationship.

NESBITT. Relationship! Don't gimme that. Whit kinna talk's that, for Christ's sake. We're punters! Punters . . . (*Taking her hand*) . . . don't get relationships, we have marriage.

MARY. (*Rising.*) No, Rab. We *had* marriage. From this moment on, I'm using the past tense. You'll never change, will you?

NESBITT. Whit'd yi mean? Whit'd yi mean?

MARY. You'll aye be the same. Living your life by the three R's. Rage, ringworm, and roll ups! Well, that's not enough for me any more, Rab Nesbitt. Coz from now on, I want the fourth R.

NESBITT. What's that?

MARY. Respectability.

Spare rib, is it? It'll be cracked rib if yi ever stick yir arse over this doorstep again!

NESBITT. (*Proffering.*) Would you settle for a packet of Revels?

MARY. Stick your sweeties. I don't know what smells worse. Our marriage or the bliddy sausages. I'm off.

She goes.

NESBITT. (*Shouting after her.*) Well go well! And bliddy good riddance! I'm tired of carrying you on my back! (*Strolling across the floor.*) They're all the same, all the same.

BURNEY. Allow you, eh Da. You handled that brilliant. You've certainly got a way with the chicks, eh?

Nesbitt scuds him, snatches gun.

NESBITT. Shuttit you!

Takes aim at Mary's picture.

. . . Who needs her? (*Shoots, hits.*) Bitch . . .!

13

SCENE 3. Pub.

Nesbitt, Jamesie, Dodie and Andra, standing at bar. Dougie is serving.

JAMESIE. Respectability. That's a terrible thing to ask from any man, Rab.

NESBITT. That's what I says to her, Jamesie. That's how I telt her straight. I'm a will 'o the wisp. A crazy kinna guy, know? I'm not the kinna man that can be shackled.

DODIE. Have you ever been shackled, Rab?

NESBITT. No.

DODIE. I have. It's pure brand new so it is. I got shackled a few times when I was on shore leave in the Navy, know?

They look at him.

DODIE. Sorry, Rab. I interrupted. On you go.

NESBITT. All's I'm saying is, that's the whole point about the bints, boy. It's the nest-building instinct! It's the nest-building! I mean, ask yi, left to his ain devices, what does the average bloke need, eh?

ANDRA. Nothin'! We're hunters! All's we need's the jungle, a cave, and a dirty big club in our hands.

JAMESIE. You're right! That's all we need! Except for maybes a nice three piece suite, and central heating on the white meter.

DODIE. Aye. And thae chinzy bedroom curtains that's out noo, with the matching valances. Have yeez seen thame?

JAMESIE AND ANDRA. Naw . . .

DODIE. Pure gallus, so they are. Come roon oors later. I'll show yi the lovely pelmet I put up.

JAMESIE AND ANDRA. We will, we will . . .

NESBITT. (*Slamming down glass.*) There y'are. Yeez see what I mean! What the hell's happening to us all these days?

DODIE. It's the new man, Rab. Adapt or die. (*Calling.*) Hey Dougie! Donnez moi a wee skoosh of Evian in there, wid yi?

DOUGIE. (*Doing so.*) You know your trouble, Nesbitt? Special pleading. Just coz your marriage broke up, you're trying to make the rest of us feel guilty.

NESBITT. Not at all! Listen pal! I'm a waster! My father before me was a waster! And there's not a wumman alive, the wumman's not been born yet that'll turn me into a respectable working man!

He goes to a table. Jamesie sighs, follows. Nesbitt, seated, takes the O.H.M.S. letter from his pocket, opens it.

JAMESIE. (*Sits.*) Rab, you and I understand each other. We're scum. And as scum, I have to tell you, you float right to the top of the sump pit.

NESBITT. Thanks, Jamesie. That means a lot to me.

JAMESIE. That's awright big man. But all I'm saying's this. I know you were born to be a waster. On a good day, you could waste for Scotland. But listen, Rab. Is it worthwhile sacrificing your marriage for your career?

NESBITT. That's a helluva decision right enough, Jamesie. But I maybes not even get the chance to make it. Listen to this. It's fae the S.S. (*Reads.*) Dear Sir . . . A knighthood, eh . . . Dear Sir, you will neither work nor want. Either take a job or we stop your dosh. Come in the morra, or else. Love, The Government. I'm paraphrasing, Jamesie, but basically that's the gist of it.

JAMESIE. Christ Almighty, Rab. It's not been your day, has it?

NESBITT. It has not, Jamesie, no. (*He cocks an ear.*)

JAMESIE. What's the matter, Rab?

NESBITT. I'm waiting for the third thing, Jamesie. You know what they say. Bad luck aye comes in threes.

Door opens. Hosie enters, looks about, spots Nesbitt.

HOSIE. Hey, Rab! Have you left your two boys in to get their ain supper?

NESBITT. Aye. How?

HOSIE. Well, you'd better get back there pronto. I think they're burning the hoose doon!

NESBITT. (*Sighs, relieved.*) Thank Christ for that. I thought he was gonny tell me some tube had left my pigeon loft open.

Nesbitt drains his glass.

SCENE 4. The Nesbitts' house. Evening.
Fire engine outside door. Firemen have just put out fire. Dripping hoses are being recoiled, etc. Gash and Burney lounging at door. Nesbitt strolls up.

NESBITT. (*To fireman.*) Awright there, pal. Yeez've got a nice night for it, in't yeez? (*To Gash and Burney.*) Whit've youse two been up to?

BURNEY. It wisnae my fault, Da. It was him. He started dabbling with the unknown.

NESBITT. Whit'd yi mean, whit'd yi mean?

BURNEY. He wanted to fun oot how the cooker worked.

GASH. Ya wee globule yi!

NESBITT. (*Scudding Gash.*) That's you all over. How may times've I telt yi never to meddle with nature?

GASH. Aya. I was just trying out my *nouvelle* cuisine.

NESBITT. That's enough. If the Good Lord had wanted us to learn *nouvelle* cuisine, he'd never have gied us crispy pancakes.

GASH. That's right, blame me! But none of this would've happened if you hadn't acted the pig with my Maw!

He storms off.

NESBITT. (*To audience.*) Weans, eh. Fair know how to twist the knife, don't they? Normally I'd rip his spleen out and stuff it doon a stank for cheek like that. But the wee keech's right, and I know it. So what else can I do. Eh? I'll show yi.

He scuds Burney across the head.

BURNEY. Aya! What was that for?

NESBITT. Nothing. But I've got to hit something, hiven't I?

BURNEY. (*Rubbing his ear, points.*) Aye, you're awfa smart now ya big swine. But just wait till you get your heart disease. (*Makes a fist.*) I'm gonny bliddy well kill you . . . !

For a smoother, fuller, more satisfying cigarette move on down to rickets country.

Burney goes, rubbing his ear.

NESBITT. (*To audience.*) (*Chuckling.*) See that, eh? That's my boy! That's my boy . . .!

SCENE 5. The Job Centre. Day.
Nesbitt sitting, waiting to be dealt with.

NESBITT. (*To audience.*) Work, eh. What a stupid way to earn a living. Christ, every bugger I know that's in work is up to the eyes in debt. So am I right enough, but at least my time's my ain to express myself.

A clerk at a desk calls him.

CLERK. (*Calling.*) Mr Nesbitt.

NESBITT. At's me pal. Here I come . . .

Nesbitt sits opposite the clerk.

NESBITT. Awright, sonny boy (*Indicates.*) Take a seat. (*Lounges back.*) Now what can I do for yi?

CLERK. You can show me some respect for a start. Now I see from your files that you haven't worked for some time, Mr Nesbitt. Why is that?

NESBITT. Well, to tell you the truth, pal. I did apply for a vacancy a wee while back there. But when I got there the job had already been filled, know?

CLERK. And what job was that?

NESBITT. King. I widnae mind, but the block that got it abdicated five minutes later too. Women trouble, know? At's the story of my life too, by the way. Yi merrit yourself, son?

CLERK. That's neither here nor there, Mr Nesbitt.

NESBITT. Aye, awright, awright . . . Just making conversation.

CLERK. (*Perusing document.*) In fact the more I study your record, the more clear it becomes that you and the concept of work have been less than intimately involved down the years. And that's a situation that's going to have to change.

NESBITT. Chinge. How? Whit for?

CLERK. Everybody has to work, Mr Nesbitt. Or do you disagree?

NESBITT. Of course I disagree. Christ Almight, there's a working population in this country of twenty million. And thur only seventeen million jobs to go roon. So some poor swines've got to be on the dole. So it might as well be them that likes it. And I lap it up like a dummy tit in Ostermilk, let me tell you that, boy.

CLERK. I'm afraid the system doesn't work that way. We must all pull our weight in life. (*Sliding over a form.*) Here's a list of Community Enterprise vacancies. You're to choose one, now, or forfeit your benefit.

NESBITT. I don't want a job. I don't want a job!

CLERK. We all must do things we don't want to do in life.

NESBITT. (*Mimics.*) 'We all must do things we don't want to do in life.' (*Pointing.*) Here, gie's that one as well! (*Notices.*) Wait a minute. Christ, is that all the dosh you're paying? (*Slinging back form.*) Why don't you just black me up and make me pick cotton and be done with it . . . !

CLERK. Thank you, Mr Nesbitt. We'll be getting in touch.

NESBITT. Och . . . Bugger aff ya wee prick!

Nesbitt exits.

SCENE 6. Outside the Job Centre. Day.
Nesbitt appears. Burney is standing, waiting.

BURNEY. Well, Da. What happened? How'd yi get on?

NESBITT. Bad news, son. I got a job.

BURNEY. Ach well, never mind Da. There's good news too.

NESBITT. Where's Gash?

BURNEY. That's the good news. He's pissed of to my Granny's. He wants to live with my Maw.

NESBITT. I see, I see. It's like that is it? It's like that. One by one they're deserting me, eh. Well, that's it then, in't it? It's just you and me against the world, Burney son. It's just like *Kramer versus Kramer*, int'it?

BURNEY. Aye. Except Meryl Streep had a bigger chist than my Maw.

NESBITT. Don't you worry, son. You want a big chest, you'll get a big chest.

He shows a breast through his string vest.

There. Can Meryl Streep beat that, eh?

BURNEY. At's what I admire about you, Da. You're all things to all men.

NESBITT. (*Ruffling Burney's hair.*) You better believe it, son. You better believe it, son.

They walk away up the street.

SCENE 7. The bus queue. Day.
The same people as before waiting for the bus. Nesbitt is now in the queue, wearing a tie, and carrying a haversack.

NESBITT. (*To audience.*) Look at me! Look at the state of me! I'm mortified! This is what the system does to yi! It takes your life, and it gies yi threepence! Look at them too. All those smiling coupons, all gloating at me.

The man in queue (from scene 1) is smirking at Nesbitt. Nesbitt glares at him.

NESBITT. What're you looking at? Say one word and I'll stiffen yi!

The bus arrives.

WOMAN IN QUEUE. (*To Nesbitt.*) Here's your bus. If you get off at the Ministry and turn left, it'll take you straight to the gates of the labour camp.

Sniggering from the queue.

NESBITT. Aye, go ahead, laugh! Laugh! But I'll tell yeez one thing! I maybe a wage slave, but I'll never be an Uncle Tom. It'll be Spartacus Nesbitt! Spartacus Nesbitt! I'll walk alone.

DRIVER. Aye, and you're gonny have to walk if you've not got wee'er than that, pal. We don't gie change on these buses.

The queue gets on the bus. Nesbitt stands, fuming.

MAN IN QUEUE. (*Getting on.*) I'm Spartatcus. . .

WOMAN IN QUEUE. No, I'm Spartacus . . .

The bus drives off and Nesbitt is left standing, still fuming.

SCENE 8. A wide open space. Day.
A wide open space. Nesbitt gazing out, soulfully. We don't see what he's gazing at yet.

NESBITT. I'll tell you one thing about me. See me. See the sea. I love the sea, me. See when you stand looking out at it, makes yi feel humble, know. That's how I picked this job, for the humility.

Pull out to show him by a park boating pond. Some kids are about to get into a boat. He whacks it with a stick.

(*Whacking.*) The red boat! I says the red boat! That's the blue boat! Do as you're telt! Wee crud!

They get into the blue boat. Nesbitt approaches Jamesie, who's sitting on a bench.

Work

JAMESIE. (*Wine bottle to hand.*) Being single doesni suit you, Rab. You're turning awffy crabbit these days.

NESBITT. Garbage! I'm as sweet natured as ever I was! (*To Burney.*) What's up with your face?

BURNEY. These pieces, Da. They're minging! (*Inspecting.*) Where'd yi get the filling? Scrape it off the sole of your shoe?

NESBITT. (*Scudding him.*) You don't know what's good for yi! That's dripping and Marmite. We were reared on that, weren't we Jamesie?

JAMESIE. Aye, Rab. Yesterday, when we were young. (*Swigs.*) Thur a lot of British sherry flowed out of the close since then though, eh?

NESBITT. (*Swigs.*) Aye, you're right there, Jamesie boy!

JAMESIE. I seen Mary the day, Rab.

NESBITT. (*Choking.*) Mary. Did she speak?

JAMESIE. Kinda, Rab. She said 'Hullo'.

NESBITT. Aye, but what I mean is, was there an undercurrent, Jamesie? Was it like 'Hullo', but secretly she was saying, 'I ache for Big Rab and I'd take him back like a shot if only he'd say the word.' Was it one of thae hullos?

JAMESIE. No, Rab. I think it was just 'Hullo'.

NESBITT. The bitch . . . !

Burney is standing, still holding his sandwich. He looks at a dog turd on the ground. He gets down, sniffs the turd. He then sniffs the sandwich. He chucks the sandwich into the pond. Nesbitt boots him on the bum.

NESBITT. Whit's your gemme, boy? You trying to say I keep a durty hoose or something? Away hame, gawn. (*Booting.*) Gawn . . . !

BURNEY. I'm going. I'm going. Aya!

Jamesie shudders.

NESBITT. (*Returning to Jamesie.*) Weans, eh Jamesie?

JAMESIE. Aye, Rab. Look, Rab. I'm not trying to interfere nor nothing.

NESBITT. I know that, Jamesie, nae bother.

JAMESIE. I mean, you know that to me, marriage is a sacred institution.

NESBITT. Oh, I know. I know. I mean, you go to confession religiously whenever you've knocked hell out of Ella.

JAMESIE. Exactly, Rab. And that's because I'm more sensitive than you. Believe me, Rab. I understand women. I know their needs. Sometimes they need a right good gubbing and other times they need romance, know?

NESBITT. Romance. I gied the bitch romance! I've never once come back from that chip shop without saving her the skin off my fish supper. (*He rakes in his pocket.*) See, look, I've even got one here.

JAMESIE. I know that, Rab. And greater love hath no block. But today's wumman wants more than the skin of a fish supper, Rab. She wants to be wooed.

NESBITT. Wooed?

JAMESIE. Aye, you know. Hearts and flowers and all that crap with maybe a cake of tablet flung in. Like I say, Rab, and I don't want to interfere. But if you want Mary back, you'll get yourself roon there to her mother's pronto and gie her a right good wooing.

NESBITT. I see, I see . . .

JAMESIE. Coz Rab, I'm sentimental. I hate fur to see something beautiful dying. I'd hate to see the bond atween two dear friends pulled asunder. And I'm not only speaking as your best man here, Rab. I'm also speaking as your pools agent. I didn't want to bring this up Rab, but since Mary went, you owe me three weeks.

NESBITT. You'll get your money, you'll get your money!

JAMESIE. Tell yi what, Rab. Will I go roon there and gie her door a knock? Mary'll listen to me.

Who am I to disturb the universe?

NESBITT. (*Jumping up.*) No! Never! Don't you dare! Because I'll tell you this, boy! She's away and she can stay away! I don't want her back! Rab C. Nesbitt begs for no wumman! No wumman!

JAMESIE. Suit yourself, Rab. If that's the way you want it, I'll not go against your wishes. (*Looks.*) Anyway, here's your gaffer coming. I'd better shoot the craw.

NESBITT. Aye, beat it, gawn . . .

Jamesie goes, hurriedly.

(*To audience, leaning on broom.*) Did yi see that there? Di yi see the flyness of me. (*Mimics Jamesie.*) 'I'll not go against your wishes, Rab'. I know fine well he'll be right roon there giving it the big licks with the sweetie mooth pronto. But that suits me fine, by the way. Suits me fine! Softens her up a bit, know? That way, she'll be ready to just melt into my erms when I make seductive overtures at getting her arse back in the cowp, know?

23

Coz that's how you've got to play it with the bints, boy. Don't bow the knee! Don't bow the knee to them!

The woman from the bus queue, now in uniform, leans out from a small Parks Department van. She shouts at Nesbitt.

WOMAN IN QUEUE. Hey, Nesbitt!! I thought I told you to get those leaves swept up! Shake a leg, pronto!

NESBITT. (*Doing so.*) Shaking it, boss. I'm shaking it . . . ! (*To audience.*) Awright, fair enough, maybes shake a leg. But don't bow the knee . . .

Toot on van horn.

. . . Brushing, boss, I'm brushing . . .

SCENE 9. A supermarket. Day.
Nesbitt with trolley. He goes to pick the bottom tin from the display. Uses his common sense and picks a tin from the top. He then turns the trolley, clumsily, and knocks down the whole display.

NESBITT. (*To audience.*) I'll tell you one thing, boy. I'm bliddy seek being a wumman, your life's never your ain. You need to keep your heid full of junk the whole time. 'Whit's the weather like, is it a good drying day?' 'Whit'll I get for the night's tea?' (*Picks up an item from the freezer, studies it.*) Look at this, eh. Feeds a family of four. Four what? Four white mice, maybes. Sell by May 9th. Tell yi one thing. Its sell-by date might not be up. But it's long past it's thieve-by date, know what I mean?

Nesbitt stuffs the item into his coat and joins the checkout queue.

NESBITT. Look at this. Right scunner, in't it, eh? Hey, whit's the hold up here? Whit's the hold up! (*Shouts, pointing.*) Right, who's all paying by cheque. Come on, who? (*Hands go up, sheepishly.*) Right, start getting them wrut out now well. Come on, write! Pronto!

They do so.

I've not got time to be stuck in queues, boy. I'm a wan parent family that's just back from his work! (*To audience.*) Hear that? I've waited all my life to say that. Whit are you looking at? (*Scanning cheques.*) Get that date in! Get the date in, pronto! (*To audience.*) Even us scruff's got to make our time cost effective . . .

Work

SCENE 10. The Nesbitts' living room.
Nesbitt arrives home.

NESBITT. (*Throwing open door, carrier bags in hand.*) Burney, son! Where are yi! Mammy's back! I've got a surprise for the night's tea! (*Squirming.*) Yi need to eat it oot my trooser leg! Burney . . . !

He notices a letter on the table.

What's this?

Picks it up, reads.

'Dear Da, this pen is running oot, so I will lean extra hard on it, so's you can read the imprint off the . . . (*looks*) . . . table. (*Reading imprint.*) See you? See your cooking? It is puke, by the way. So I am off . . . (*running out of table*) to live at my Granny's. Also you are running out of . . . continued inside food cabinet . . .

He opens a door on the food cabinet. Corn Flakes cascade out from an open box that has been propped up cunningly.

(*reading.*) . . . Cornflakes . . .

An arrow on the cabinet points towards the work top, directly below the cabinet. Nesbitt sweeps a clearing in the cornflakes, reads the worktop.

(*Reading.*) Awrabest, Burney . . .

Nesbitt sits heavily.

(*To audience.*) Whit'd yi make of that then, eh? (*Emotionally.*) And I'd just got him a four-pack of Carly specials too, for failing all his 'O' level prelims . . .

He sits, cradling the four-pack, lip trembling.

. . . (*In a croak, singing.*) Ali Bali, Ali Bali Bee, sitting on yir Daddy's knee . . .

SCENE 11. Mary's mother's house. Night.
Mary's parents sit silent, immobile, watching the television.

Jamesie is pleading on Nesbitt's behalf. Mary is attempting to be strong but is in grave danger of weakening. Jamesie rests his hand on hers.

JAMESIE. You want to see him, Mary hen. It's pathetic, so it is.

25

MARY. How'd yi mean?

JAMESIE. He's . . . respectable, Mary. He gets up in the morning, gets shaved, goes to his work. Comes back at night, watches the telly, and has a quiet pint on a Saturday night.

MARY. That doesnie sound like Rab.

JAMESIE. No. See, since you left him, he's gone right uphill. It's tragic, Mary. But that's respectability for you. It does terrible things to a man.

They look at Mary's parents. Mary's mother switches off the telly.

MOTHER. Ah well, nine o'clock. Time for bed, mister.

FATHER. Aye, that's another day in, Mother. Not long now till we take the long dark journey into death.

MOTHER. (*Excited.*) No . . . !

FATHER. Quietly Mother. Show some restraint. Enthusiasm is common.

MOTHER. Right, Father . . .

They go, arm in arm, po-faced. Mary and Jamesie shudder.

MARY. (*To Jamesie.*) Aye, that's all very well, Jamesie. But Rab brung all this on himself. If he's turning respectable, that's not my fault. For years he's taken our marriage for granted. Now, he's paying the price.

JAMESIE. Aye, and what a price it is, Mary hen. Honestly if you could just see his face.

MARY. What about his face?

BURNEY. (*Entering.*) It's like an arse with a hangover.

MARY. Shuttit you! (*To Jamesie.*) Look, don't tell me any more, it's just upsetting me. If Rab wants me back he can do his ain asking. I'm sick fed up of cow-towing whenever it suits him. (*Storming off.*) Let him try sooking up to me for a change!

She exits, slamming into Gash at the door. She gives him a clout.

GASH. Aya! What was that for?

MARY. (*Blurst it out.*) For having your faither's eyes . . . !

26

Work

SCENE 12. The Nesbitts' living room. Night.
Nesbitt and Jamesie are in the living room. Jamesie is sitting. Nesbitt is using a carpet sweeper with difficulty. Empty tins, papers, bags, etc. litter the carpet.

He runs the sweeper over the carpet. It deposits a wedge of fluffy dirt. He runs it back again. The fluffy dirt remains. He shakes the sweeper, kicks it.

NESBITT. Take her back, is it? Take her back! Never! Ten thousand times never! Well, maybes. How, whit'd she say, Jamesie?

JAMESIE. Well, like I says Rab, I just heard through the grapevine like. From a wee mate's uncle's sister's pal, that kinna thing. I says you widnae be interested like. (*Removing a tin from underneath him.*) I says you were getting on fine without her.

NESBITT. You're bliddy right, boy. Wumman, is it? Wumman! Christ, I'm a better wumman than she'll ever be. And I'm a man. In fact, see if I wisnae married, I'd invite myself away for a dirty weekend!

JAMESIE. I see. (*Half rising.*) Well, I'll put the word out then that you're not interested, eh Rab?

NESBITT. Hod on, hod on! Me and you go back a long way, am I right, Jamesie?

JAMESIE. You speak the truth, Rab.

NESBITT. And to blocks of our generation, marriage is a sacred institution, is it not?

JAMESIE. That is correct, Rab.

NESBITT. So, if the soor faced slag wants to come back to me, it's only right that I should listen, is it not?

JAMESIE. See you, Rab Nesbitt. You're a prince amongst men. In fact, you're better than that. (*Punching him playfully.*) You're no' a bad fella!

NESBITT. (*Reciprocating the punch.*) And you're no' a bad fella tae, Jamesie!

They hug, Jamesie turns to go.

(*Calling after him.*) And remember, Jamesie. This is personal. Not a word to nobody, yi hear?

JAMESIE. Rab, I'd sooner have my sex organs pickled in vinegar!

He exits.

NESBITT. (*To audience.*) There'll be some queer seafood roon the pubs of Govan this weekend . . .

SCENE 13. Outside Mary's mother's house. Night.
Back green of a block of council flats. A light lattice fence separates the blocks. Nesbitt stands, looking up at a bedroom window.

NESBITT. (*Shouts.*) Mary! Mary! (*To audience.*) Look at the state of me, eh? I huvnie done this for a while. In fact, see if she flung me doon a piece on sugar, it'd be like being a ten-year-old again.

A half-hidden female face appears at the window.

NESBITT. (*Shouts up.*) Mary darling, is that you?

FACE. (*Shouts down.*) Aye, Rab, it's me. Whit is it you're wanting?

NESBITT. I want you Mary! (*Emotional.*) You're my wife! I want you back! Life's not the same withoot yi!

FACE. I see. Well, if I did come back, things would have to change.

NESBITT. Name it Mary. I'll do what yi want! Just come back to me in the namea Christ, come back!

FACE. Right. Well, first of all, I want a rise in my housekeeping.

NESBITT. I don't gie you any housekeeping.

FACE. Exactly Rab. It's got to change.

NESBITT. Awright, awright. What else?

FACE. Then I want you to be nicer to the weans.

NESBITT. The weans.

SCENE 14. Bedroom. Night.
We see Burney, in drag, at the window. Gash is squatting beside him, out of sight.

BURNEY. Aye, especially Burney . . . aya!

Gash has kicked him.

GASH. (*Mutters.*) Aye, yi had to get that in, didn't yi?

BURNEY. (*Mutters back.*) Natch! Who's in the front line here? Watch this, I'll stitch him up with this one.

SCENE 15. Outside Mary's mother's house. Night.
Nesbitt is still standing in the garden, shouting up.

NESBITT. Okay, I'll be nicer to the weans! What else?

BURNEY. (*Shouts down.*) I want sexual satisfaction ten times a week.

GASH. With matinees on Sunday!

A snorting noise from behind the lattice fence. Nesbitt looks. A light is switched on in the bedroom. He looks up. Mary appears at the window.

MARY. (*At window, scudding Burney.*) Get in there you. And whit've I told you about dressing up in my claes! Ya wee perv!

Nesbitt watches her knuckle them away from the window. Realisation dawns.

NESBITT. Cotter . . . !

He stomps towards the fence, rips out a section. Behind it squats Jamesie, Dodie and Andra. Jamesie is speaking authoritatively to Andra and Dodie.

JAMESIE. (*Prodding the earth.*) So, plant your bulbs in May or June, in a good mulchy soil . . . (*Looking up, innocently.*) . . . Oh, hullo, Rab. Did you want to join wur gardening club?

Nesbitt sticks a plant pot over Jamesie's head.

NESBITT. No! (*To Dodie and Andra.*) Do youse want the same . . . !

DODIE. (*In appeasement, Bill and Ben.*) Flubadub, big man. Nae messin . . .

Dodie and Andra leg it.

NESBITT. (*Shouting after them.*) Weeds . . . !

SCENE 16. The supermarket. Day.
Nesbitt is in the checkout queue.

Rab C. Nesbitt

NESBITT. (*To audience.*) Christ, it just goes to show, din't it, eh? Yi never know what's ahead of yi. One week you're cock of the walk, getting breast fed at the bosom of your nuclear family, and the next they've cut your progeny off and you're queueing up with a mincy wee basket getting frozen dinners for one. (*Holds up packet.*) Look at this crap, eh. More tasty treats from the Birdy's Eye losers range. (*To man next to him.*) It's not fun living on your jack, is it pal?

MAN. Don't worry. It gets better when you start talking to yurself. Then at least you've got a wee bit of company, know?

The man resumes gibbering to himself. Nesbitt unloads his groceries onto the conveyor belt.

NESBITT. (*To assistant.*) Hey, hen. I'm helpless. Fancy mothering me?

No response. A familiar voice speaks.

MARY. It's not a mother you want. It's a wet nurse.

NESBITT. Mary.

MARY. (*Lifting items.*) What are you getting this for? Since when did you like powdered milk?

NESBITT. (*Laying a hand on hers.*) Since you left me, doll. I sook it off my dental plate in the wee sma' hours. It saves me getting night starvation, know?

MARY. (*Lifting another tin.*) And what's this? We're not paying that. We'll get their ain make. It's three pence cheaper.

NESBITT. 'We', Mary. Did you say 'we'?

MARY. Are you deaf as well as glaiket?

NESBITT. (*To assistant.*) Here, doll! Yi can ring this through an all!

He opens his coat with a flourish, produces a chicken.

To hell, I'm gonny pay for it. I feel like celebrating.

MARY. (*To queue, chuffed.*) Did yeez all hear that? And he husnie even got a drink in him . . .

She gives him a squeeze. A bottle drops from Nesbitt's coat, breaks.

... Awright, but perfection's boring ... !

SCENE 17. The park. Day.
At the park. Nesbitt is by the pond, spiking leaves.

NESBITT. (*To audience.*) Tell yeez wan thing though. Nest building is it? Burds is it? Work is it? You can stuff the lot of it. Coz, see when yi get right down to it, blocks is the real gentle sex. We're simple sowels. Gie us a hot dinner at one end, and a warm gun at the other end, and we're as happy as pigs in glabber. But, bints, boy. See bints. They're only saft on the ootside. See on the inside, they've got hearts on them as hard as Hygena worktops.

A van horn sounds. We see the boss woman (woman in bus queue) in her van.

NESBITT. (*Spiking furiously.*) Aye, I'm grafting. Look at me. I'm grafting. (*To audience.*) It's the benefit of the doubt, awright, calling that yin a chick. I'll not tell yi what kinna burd she is, but she's got a fur collar growing round her neck.

The boss woman approaches.

WOMAN IN QUEUE. Nesbitt! Nesbitt!

NESBITT. (*To audience.*) She's gonny get it! I'm telling yi, bliddy earth mother or no!

WOMAN IN QUEUE. Are you still at it? (*Kicking pile.*) How long does it take you to sweep up a few leaves for goodness' sake?

NESBITT. It's not my fault! (*Waving his arms about.*) It's Mother Nature! It's Nature!! It's the wind. Blowing about, giving it the dirty big waft, (*leaping about the pile.*) Christ, if I ston this side, it blaws roon the other side. And if I ston the other side, it swerves roon my khyber and scatters the bliddy lot! What can I dae? What can I dae? I am just a man. Naked came I into the world, and in a string semmit I'll go out of it! Who am I to disturb the Universe.

WOMAN IN QUEUE. I see. Well, Nesbitt, if you can't do the job maybe I should get someone else who can.

NESBITT. (*To audience, defeated.*) I'll tell yeez wan thing. It's just as well I had my weans afore I came into this job. Coz I sure as Christ wouldn't have the toy dolls for it afterwards.

Win a luxury weekend for two in Govan! Simply arrange these fizzogs in order of ugliness and complete the following sentence: 'I love poverty because . . . ?' (No more than two words.)

Mary approaches, carrying a sandwich box.

MARY. Here y'are, Rab. I've brung your pieces. You forgot them.

WOMAN IN QUEUE. He won't have time to eat those. He's got far too much work to do.

MARY. No? Who says?

WOMAN IN QUEUE. I do. I am an area administrator in the Parks and Amenities Department. And, effectively your husband's employer. I say.

MARY. I see. Well, look. I'm just a housewife. I don't have a big career or the fancy talk nor nothing like that. So I widnae even attempt to argue with yi.

WOMAN IN QUEUE. Good.

MARY. No. So, instead I'll just get right down to it. And give your the severe malky.

She nuts the woman. The woman falls into the pond.

NESBITT. Mary, Mary! What are you doing? That's my job!

MARY. Rab, please! Ours is a modern marriage. We share the work load.

NESBITT. (*To audience.*) See that, eh? What a woman. She's got me spoiled rotten, so she has.

They go, arm in arm. Gash joins them.

NESBITT. (*Voice over.*) Aye, see when yi get right down to it. I've got a lot to be thankful for. I'm the man with everything. Good wife, (*Ruffles Gash's hair*) fine son, and my ain wee pet animal.

Nesbitt picks up a stick, flings it.

There y'are, Burney son! Fetch! Fetch!

BURNEY. (*Seated.*) Get it yourself ya stookie. You flung it . . . (*Gets a kick*) Awright, I'm gawn da, I'm gawn . . . (*To audience.*) Might as well humour the tube. He'll be a long time deid.

The family, strolling through the park. Burney running, back and forwards, fetching the stick.

Rab C. Nesbitt

EPISODE TWO

CAST LIST

STEVEN, THE CANVASSER	Simon Donald
GAVIN CLARK	Kenny Ireland
MINISTER	Supporting artist
RAB C. NESBITT	Gregor Fisher
FIRST POLLSTER	Libby McArthur
SECOND POLLSTER	Stuart Henderson
HUGH HOSIE	Jake D'Arcy
DODIE	Iain McColl
JAMESIE COTTER	Tony Roper
ANDRA	Brian Pettifer
DOUGIE	Charlie Sim
MARY NESBITT	Elaine C. Smith
GASH	Andrew Fairlie
BURNEY	Eric Cullen
SNP CANDIDATE	Ron Donachie
GIFT SHOP CUSTOMER	Claire Neilson
GIFT SHOP ASSISTANT	Juliet Cadzow
RETURNING OFFICER	John Shedden
CLATTY McCUTCHEON	David McNiven

Rat

SCENE 1. A street in Govan. Day.
A van in Labour Party colours, driving up a dismal street in Govan. A megaphone sounds: 'Vote for Gavin Clark, your Labour Party candidate on the sixteenth of May. That's Gavin Clark . . .' etc.

There are some grotesque low-life types, sitting on the front steps, shoogling prams backwards and forwards, smoking, etc, idly watching the van pass.

The driver, (Steven the canvasser) is the one who's doing the talking into the megaphone. Gavin Clark, the politician, sits next to him with his hands over his eyes.

STEVEN. (*Through megaphone.*) That's Gavin Clark, your Labour candidate . . . (*To Clark.*) . . . Well, we're here. Govan South. The clogged artery in the heartland of punterdom. You'd better open your eyes and take a look at it.

GAVIN CLARK. Do I have to?

STEVEN. I think it's only fair. Seeing as how you're hoping to be Member of Parliament for the area.

GAVIN CLARK. Not for long I hope. I aim to move on to far bigger things.

STEVEN. What? The Cabinet?

GAVIN CLARK. Are you kidding? I want a chat show on cable telly. Or maybe my own column in the *Sun*. You forget, Steven, I rose from this sump pit. (*Points.*) You see that window up there?

STEVEN. Yes.

GAVIN CLARK. I was born in that den.

STEVEN. Really? I wonder if it's changed much.

GAVIN CLARK. I shouldn't think so. It's still got the same egg box section covering the broken pane.

We see the broken window.

STEVEN. You're very cynical aren't you? D'you really think there's nothing we can do for places like South Govan then?

GAVIN CLARK. Oh, aye! We could cash in on the leisure boom. Throw a fence around it and turn it into a safari park. The place is full of bears anyway.

STEVEN. Bears, Gavin? What's a bear then?

GAVIN CLARK. A bear? It's hard to explain. But put it this way. You'll know one when you see one.

Jamesie, rounding a corner into view, unaware. He looks furtive, hiding something under his jacket.

STEVEN. (*Pointing.*) Look! Look! Is that one there?

Jamesie is startled. He darts back round the corner, out of view.

GAVIN CLARK. (*Looking out.*) Where? Where?

STEVEN. He was there a second ago. Then he sort of darted into the undergrowth!

GAVIN CLARK. Yes, they're deeply suspicious creatures. You'd think we were out to steal their souls or something, rather than just trying to tease their votes. (*Shuddering.*) Och, come on, let's lunch at Emilio's. Get me out of this graveyard . . . !

They drive off, fast.

SCENE 2. A graveyard. Day.
A burial service by an open grave. A few mourners, a Minister saying a few words as the pall bearers prepare to lower a coffin.

MINISTER. For Jesus said, I am the resurrection and the light, whomsoever believeth in me shall have everlasting . . .

The pall bearers stand poised to lower the coffin. A shout is heard.

NESBITT. Haw! Haw! Whit's the score and that?

He pops up from the grave.

(*To pall bearers.*) Youse want to watch what you're doing with that thing! Yi could kill soembody with that! (*To Minister.*) And you, boy, I'm surprised at you. did you not know there's a by-election on? One man, one grave, by the way.

He climbs out.

(*To mourners.*) There y'are, dolls, no offence. Yeeze can have it back now, I'm finished with it. And I'll tell yeez wan thing, I pity him in the box, coz it's not a patch on a Slumberland, by the way . . . !

There is no response.

36

Rat

Another venture into the labour market. I find work as a singing death-o-gram.

(*Going.*) Ach, suit yirsels . . . (*To audience, stretching his back.*) Tell yi something. Yi don't half fall asleep in some queer places when you're drunk, eh?

He walks on a couple of yards, discovers a substantial length of car exhaust, picks it up.

Namea God, look at that, eh. That'll come in hand that. Must've fell of the back of a hearse. Better than some of the things that could've fell off, I suppose!

By Christ, I'm in some form the day awright!

Wandering off, trailing the exhaust.

Must've got oot the right side of bed for once . . .

SCENE 3. A Govan street. Day.
Nesbitt walking along a Govan street, trailing the exhaust. A van, in SNP colours drives past, blaring 'Scotland the Brave'.

NESBITT. (*To audience.*) Tell yi something else. It's not just me. See with this by-election, there's quite a few things crawled out from under the grun, by the way.

Pollster approaches him. Clipboard in hand.

FIRST POLLSTER. Excuse me, can I just ask you, how will you be voting in the by-election?

NESBITT. (*Without stopping.*) Communist! Without a doubt! (*To audience.*) Tell them anything, shuts them up.

He gets a few yards. A second pollster stops him.

SECOND POLLSTER. Excuse me, how are you going to vote in the by-election?

NESBITT. Alliance! I'm a don't know. (*To audience.*) Wee bit of satire there, know?

Walks on a couple more yards. A man wearing a blue rosette confronts him, hand outstretched.

HUGH HOSIE. Good morning. I'm Hugh Hosie, your Conservative candidate. Can I rely on your vote at the by-election?

NESBITT. Can yi? Get to buggery! (*To audience, walking on.*) A joke's a joke, know?

HUGH HOSIE. (*Pursuing him.*) Och, *please*, mate! *Go on* . . . be a pal!

NESBITT. (*Stopping.*) Whit?

HUGH HOSIE. Gonny vote for me, *please!* Nobody else will. I mean, what chance have I got roon here? My Mammy and all my mates is gonny be watching me on *Panorama* and I'll feel that stupid if I don't get any votes.

NESBITT. Well, that's not my fault. Yi should've thought about that afore yi pinned that bit of blue keech to your tit.

HUGH HOSIE. I know! But whit could I do, I'm just a token working class Tory. They only put me up coz it was cheaper than hiring a monkey from Edinburgh Zoo. Honest to God, Jim. I'm not a toff. I'm just a wee right wing hustler. I sell carpet offcuts up the indoor market. Look at these knuckles! (*Shows tattoos.*) I'm trash, same as yirsel!

NESBITT. That's not the point! The secret of the ballot box is between me and my conscience. That's if I happen to be conscious at the time, of course.

HUGH HOSIE. (*Taking mat from parked car.*) Here. Tell yi what. Look. If I gie yi this free doormat, will yi at least think about it? It'd mean a lot to me, pal. Means bugger all to Maggie Thatcher, but it matters to me!

NESBITT. Aye, awright, awright. I'll think aboot it, but I'm making no promises!

HUGH HOSIE. Cheers, pal. Awrabest. (*Calls after him.*) And if yi ever get any bother with your constitutional rights, you come and see me roon the carpet stall, okay?

NESBITT. (*Calls back.*) Aye, awright, awright . . . (*To audience.*) Christ, look at that, eh. Bought aff wi a doormat. I canny help feeling there's something symbolic about that. (*Yawns.*)

SCENE 4. The pub. Day.
Dougie behind counter. Andra and Dodie leaning on bar. They're watching a television set above the bar which is showing film of the by-election candidates doing the rounds, hand shaking, baby kissing, etc. Jamesie enters. Andra and Dodie look to the door.

DODIE. Hullo there, Jamesie!

JAMESIE. Hullo, boys . . .

ANDRA. What's the matter, Jamesie son? You're looking a bit flustered.

JAMESIE. (*Joining them at bar.*) Aye, and nae wonder. Have yeez been oot there lately? The joint's hoaching with media. I canny stop scratching myself. (*Doing so.*)

DODIE. (*Doing likewise.*) Well pack it in. Or you'll get us at it too.

JAMESIE. It's awright for youse. Youse wunnie followed by the Labour Party halfway up Govan Road. I was very near keeching myself. I thought they were snoopers from the SS.

ANDRA. What's that pong?

JAMESIE. Listen, I says 'very near'. I stopped short of the full article.

DODIE. Aye, but not that far short. What's that stuck doon your troosers?

JAMESIE. Nothing. (*Opens jacket to reveal fish tail sticking up.*) Just a salmon.

DOUGIE. Allow him! It pays to advertise, eh Jamesie?

JAMESIE. Listen, this is no ordinary salmon! This is a historical salmon! This is the first salmon to get caught in the River Clyde since 1896!

ANDRA. Where did yi get it?

JAMESIE. Off a block with a chip van outside Presto's.

DOUGIE. Him! Wee Clatty McCutcheon! His spins more yarns than Taiwan that yin.

DODIE. Aye, ya mug yi! (*To Dougie.*) Who's Clatty McCutcheon, by the way?

ANDRA. Wee block. One eye, one leg, plays a tin whistle. Yi must've seen him.

DODIE. Gie's a brek. Eveybody up oor street looks like that.

JAMESIE. Anyway, I don't care if it is a yarn! I want to believe it, okay! I want to believe that things is getting better! That this can be a bustling wee toon again! And that I've got the biggest

Rat

Of course the hoose has full central heating. I put it in myself you know.

salmon in Govan! And anyhow, if things urnie getting better, how comes the media's (*scratches involuntarily*) jumping aboot all ower us now, eh? Tell me that!

DOUGIE. (*Scratching.*) It's nothing personal, Jamesie. It's what's called a litmus test. They like to watch how folk vote in a by-election. It shows them how the rest of the country's thinking.

DODIE. Christ, they could've saved theirselves some bother. If they want to know how Govan's thinking, they only need to ask one man.

ANDRA. Aye, I wisht Big Rab was here now. He could sum up the whole circus in one eloquent well turned phrase . . .

SCENE 5. The Nesbitts' living room. Evening.
The television on, showing a politician. The exhaust leans against wall, Nesbitt's jacket draped from it. Nesbitt is asleep in his chair. He mutters to himself.

NESBITT. Pish . . . ! It's all pish . . . ! Don't talk to me . . . !

SCENE 6. The Nesbitt's kitchen. Evening.
Mary opens a cupboard. Junk falls out.

MARY. Bliddy junk! If it's not motor exhausts it's . . . He's got half of Govan in here. Yi never know what you're gonny . . .

She screams, horrified. Gash rushes in.

GASH. What is it, Maw? What's up?

MARY. (*Points.*) Doon there. Lookit. Oh my God . . .

We get a shot of a large rat, on the floor. Food about it.

GASH. (*Looks.*) Hullo! A bit of excitement! (*Shouts into the living room.*) Hey, Tadger! Quick! Here and see this.

Burney enters.

BURNEY. Aye, whit is it?

GASH. Look . . . !

BURNEY. That's nice. What're you going to call it, Maw?

MARY. (*Skiting him.*) I'm not calling it anything! It's a rat, in't it, it's not a pet! Where's your Da?

BURNEY. Watching the by-election special . . .

SCENE 7. The Nesbitts' living room. Evening.
Nesbitt is asleep in the chair.

On the telly, the SNP candidate is speaking. We see the TV picture.

SNP CANDIDATE. And let me say this to the voters of South Govan. Don't be apathetic. Get involved. Because the greatest asset any nation has is its . . .

MARY. Remote control button . . .

She turns the set off. Shakes Nesbitt awake.

Rab! Rab! Will you wake up . . . !

NESBITT. (*Startled awake.*) Whit? Whit is it?

MARY. Help me. There's a rat in the kitchen.

NESBITT. A rat? Whit's it doing in there?

Rat

See this dug? This dug does tricks.

MARY. Well, it's not doing the washing up, I know that much. Come on, get up off your bahookey! (*Hauling him up.*) You know I've got a thing about vermin!

NESBITT. Don't I just, doll, don't I just. (*Grabbing her.*) D'yi fancy a wee dance?

MARY. (*Fighting him off.*) Never mind that ! Just get rid of it, wid yi! Things like that gie me the creeps. Christ knows where they're coming fae.

NESBITT. (*At window.*) I know fine well where they're coming fae! It's thae trendies! It's the trendies bringing them in from across the water!

MARY. Don't start that again.

NESBITT. (*Trying window.*) Has the cooncil not come about this windae yet?

43

MARY. Gie them a chance. I only rang them three year ago.

Doorbell rings. Mary opens door. Steven, the canvasser stands there.

STEVEN. Hello there. Can I just ask you if you're interested in the question of women's rights?

MARY. Oh, I don't know. I'll need to ask my man. (*Shouts.*) Hey, Rab! Am I interested in women's rights?

NESBITT. No! (*Coming to door.*) Who is it by the way? Whit'd yi want?

STEVEN. I'm here on behalf of Gavin Clark, your Labour candidate. Can we count on your vote at the by-election?

NESBITT. My vote? Whit'd yi want with that useless article?

STEVEN. Don't be cynical Mr Nesbitt. There's a lot we can do for Govan you know.

NESBITT. I see. Can you kill rats and fix windaes as well?

STEVEN. No, but . . .

NESBITT. Then you're no use to me. Bugger aff.

Goes to shut door, opens it again.

NESBITT. Hey, yi got a light there, pal?

Steven the canvasser obliges.

NESBITT. That's the gemme. *Now* bugger aff . . .

Shuts door.

(*To audience.*) See, that's my style. I make democracy work for me, know?

BURNEY. (*Shouts.*) Hey, Da! Quick! 'Mere and see this!

NESBITT. I'm coming, I'm coming!

SCENE 8. The Nesbitts' kitchen. Evening.
Close up on the rat. It wears a milk bottle top hat.

BURNEY. Look, Da! A rat in a hat!

GASH. Sitting on a mat! Pretty clever, eh Da! Witty and that!

NESBITT. (*Skiting them.*) No, it bliddy well isnae witty! Is this

If there's nae Clause Four in it, yi can
stick it up yir arse! (Although judging by the patronising expression
on his fizzer it looks as if he already has.)

how I've brung yeez up, eh? To rip the piss out of dumb
animals?

GASH. It's only a rat, Da.

NESBITT. (*Another skite.*) Shuttit you! Never forget, everyone of
us is rats, but nane of us is *only* a rat! They're maybes animals
but they've got as much right to be here as us Nesbitts. And
don't just take my word for it, read your Good Book, boy! Ask
God!

BURNEY. Hey God . . .

NESBITT. (*Another skit.*) Smart arse! Coz I'll tell you this, boy!
See the God fella, he got a hod of Adam Nesbitt right at the off,
and his says unto him: 'See thame, by the way, (*pointing at rat*)

45

thame in the fur coats, with the stupid looking faces, they are my animals, by the way! My animals. So let them go forward, and never work, and get plenty of nookie. Coz it'll make up for them having nae heaven, there y'are.'

GASH. I see. Well thanks, Da, that explains a lot.

BURNEY. Aye, cheers, Da. That's really changed my life.

NESBITT. Good! Then my living has not been vain. (*Calls.*) Hey, Mary! Where's my dinner? Is it in the micro . . . ?

MARY. (*Appearing at door.*) In the micro? You'll be bliddy lucky. You're half an hour late. Your dinner's in the rat, boy!

NESBITT. In the rat? (*Turns to rat.*) Ya verminous wee swine yi . . . !

He picks up a saucepan, batters the rat.

GASH & BURNEY. (*Together.*) Ech!

MARY. (*Arms round both.*) For behold the Lord God Nesbitt is a jealous God . . .

They look down at the rat.

SCENE 9. A trendy gift shop. Day.
In the shop there is a female assistant and a female customer.

CUSTOMER. (*Looking at one.*) These prints of the old Govan are awfully nice, aren't they, Lorna?

ASSISTANT. Yes. The barefoot bairns and the hunger marchers. They're going a bomb with all the heightened media interest. The poor were so picturesque in those days, weren't they?

Nesbitt enters. A rat tail dangles from his pocket. He listens.

CUSTOMER. Yes, not like nowadays. Where are the quaint old characters of yesteryear, eh Lorna?

ASSISTANT. Gone awa' tae bide awa', Morag. Gone awa' tae bide awa' . . . !

NESBITT. In the namea Christ . . .

ASSISTANT. Yes, can I help you?

NESBITT. No, doll, you can not. I want the top man. Where's

wee Clatty?

ASSISTANT. Clatty? If you mean Mr McCutcheon who used to own this business, I'm afraid he's gone.

NESBITT. Gone? Whit'd yi mean gone?

ASSISTANT. I mean left. Vamoosed. Sold out and upped sticks.

NESBITT. But wee Clatty was here for ower thirty year.

ASSISTANT. Yes, and it showed, believe me. (*To customer.*) The cleaning I had to do, Morag.

CUSTOMER. Oh, I know. There's no room for mockitness in modrin business, Lorna.

NESBITT. By Christ, and youse've changed your tune! One minute it's all 'Where are they now, the characters of yesteryear!' Now it's 'Get them all to buggery, the clatty animals.'

ASSISTANT. Well, now that you've got that off your chest, maybe you'd like to tell me what you're in for?

NESBITT. Certainly. I'll tell you what I'm in for. (*Holding up rat.*) Yi got any rat poison?

Customer squeals, assistant gasps.

NESBITT. What's the matter with her?

ASSISTANT. (*Comforting customer.*) There, there. (*To Nesbitt.*) Look I want you out of here! Out, before I call the police!

NESBITT. (*To customer.*) It's awright, doll, it's deid, look.

He slams the rat against the counter to prove his point. Customer squeals again.

Christ, and I thought youse'd like rats tae. Rats is the quaint old Govan, in't it, eh? (*Showing customer.*) Look, doll, clag a wee dod of hessian behind that, whap it into a frame, and you could pamp it up on your patio, next to your copper warming pan.

ASSISTANT. I said out! Now!

NESBITT. Awright, I'm gawn, I'm gawn! But I'll tell yeez wan thing. Thur were nae rats in this scheme. Not till youse trendies moved in!

Make new friends. Be popular at parties . . .

ASSISTANT. That's a terrible thing to say. No wonder the middle classes are being forced to live in ghettos.

NESBITT. Aye, and yeez can ghetto to buggery, back to where yeez came fae an' all. Who knows what bugs you people's bringing in.

ASSISTANT. That's rich! Coming from a walking midden with a tourniquet round his head!

NESBITT. Whatch your gub, doll! Don't insult our customs! This is a traditional Govan headdress! Only a chief gets to wear one of these. Heid heidbanger! And I'll tell yeez another thing . . . . (*Breaks off mid-rant, noticing.*) Is that one of thae closed circuit tellies up there, by the way?

Rat

ASSISTANT. Yes . . .

Nesbitt grins, rakishly, looking into the closed circuit screen.

NESBITT. (*To closed circuit camera.*) Hi there! I'm Rab, I'm 39 and I like to party! (*Back to ranting.*) But I'll tell yeez wan thing! Yeez'll be hearing from my solicitor, first thing in the morning!

He heads for the door.

(*To audience.*) Between you and me, I don't actually have a solicitor. I just always wanted to say that, know?

CUSTOMER. (*To assistant, shaken.*) What was all that about?

ASSISTANT. I'm not sure. I think he was searching for the secret of fire . . .

They look to the door.

SCENE 10. A supermarket. Day.
Mary walking about, pushing trolley.

MARY. (*To audience.*) Tell yi' something though. They huvnie half changed wur eating habits. See before the trendies moved in, the nearest thing this place had to a fresh vegetable was a bashed in tin of peas with fungus doon the side from where the juice had leaked out the can. Now look at it. (*We look at it.*) Yi could hide a Japanese sodjer in there . . .

Mary moves on.

Mary queueing at checkout. Mid-queue.

(*To audience.*) This is the bit I hate. It's not so much a checkout queue this, it's more the Day of Judgement. And it disnae matter how jazzy a headscarf yi wear, it disnae take the poor look away from your groceries. Know what he's getting for his tea the night? (*Shows packet.*) 'Finest escalope of veal in a delicate oriental sauce'. See if he disnae like it I'll ram it right up his artichoke, I'm telling yi. Ach, but it's my ain fault. I just didnae have the nerve to stand among this lot with a bagful of mutton pies. Yi know, I think I might have the beginnings here of an inferiority complex. (*Chuffed, as queue moves on.*) I must be a more interesting person than I thought . . .

SCENE 11. New housing estate. Day.
A trendy, new, private housing development, down by the river,

Nesbitt walking along, he waves the rat about as he speaks.

NESBITT. Look at this, eh. See this. I'm a big scum noo, but see when I was a wee scum, all this was all factories. Far as the eye could see, giving work to thoosands of men. Thank Christ them days is gone and filth like myself can sleep peaceful in wur beds in nights. At least we could till noo. (*Points at sign.*) Look at that, eh. Talk about a sign of the times. 'River Clyde Farm Estate'. Make yi laugh, eh? Know what we called this dump when we were weans? 'Rats Alley'. (*To rat.*) Aye, you're too young to remember, but your faither, he'd mind. (*To audience.*) But see the rats in thae days, they were decent rats, they were well bred, they kept theirselves to theirselves. Not like nooadays. But that's not their fault, it's society, know? Yi only get the rats yi deserve. Know who I blame? (*Makes sweeping gesture towards houses.*) These buggers here! Look at them. All the wee active citizens.

A curtain twitches.

This is the type that can get 'Four Big Helpings' out a Marks & Spencer Ocean Pie. All keeking out, all hypertense in case I break into their Ford Sierras. All keeching themselves in case I'm the start of an inflow trend. (*Stopping outside house for sale.*) Think I'll make oot I'm viewing this drum, just to gie tham all heart failure. (*Consults his* Daily Record, *looks up at house.*) Oh aye, this'll do me. Plenty of room for my tribe of weans and my bull terriers. (*To twitching curtain.*) Aye, look at me, doll! I'll neither work nor want, and this is me buying a durty big hoose! Free market! Easy! Easy!

A hand taps him on the shoulder. He turns. Gavin Clark stands, in shirt sleeves, looking annoyed. Steven sits in the van close by.

GAVIN CLARK. Look, would you mind keeping the noise down?

NESBITT. Whit'd yi mean? Whit'd yi mean?

GAVIN CLARK. Some of us have to work, you know! Some of us have to carry the flaming torch of pragmatic socialism through piss stinking low-life dunnies! And with only a measly half hour for lunch!

NESBITT. I see, I see . . .

GAVIN CLARK. And when I come home in the evening, I expect to hear nothing but the sound of silence! That's what I'm paying

Rat

poll tax for! Nothing but silence, Mozart, and the sizzle of cannelloni warming on my split level hob! I do not expect to bring work home with me! Understood!

NESBITT. Wait a minute. I know you, don't I?

GAVIN CLARK. I very much doubt it.

NESBITT. Aye, I do. You're wee Mad Mental Gavvy Clark. I used to go to school with you, mind?

GAVIN CLARK. (*Regards him.*) Nesbitt? I thought I recognised that head wound. I haven't seen you in 30 years!

NESBITT. Aye, me and you used to have ranting contests, mind?

GAVIN CLARK. Yes. I'd open for the swots in the back row, then you'd reply for the dumplings in the front!

NESBITT. Aye. Then we'd both turn blue, try to slash each other with compasses, and get dragged, kicking and swearing to the headmaster's office.

GAVIN CLARK. Yes, I was certainly different in those days.

NESBITT. Aye, you were an idealist.

GAVIN CLARK. Yes. Thank God I had that educated out of my system. All the same, I often think back to our old classmates . . . people like Jamesie . . .

NESBITT. Cotter.

GAVIN CLARK. Aye. And wee Andra . . .

NESBITT. Binnie. Andra Binnie.

GAVIN CLARK. That's it! You know, the last time I saw those guys they were propping up the bar at Howden's. And that was 25 years ago, I wonder where they are today, eh?

Knowing look from Nesbitt.

NESBITT. Tell yi what. If yi fancy nicking roon now, you'll fun out. They're still waiting on you to get your round in.

GAVIN CLARK. Go round there. I hardly think so . . .

STEVEN. (*Nudging him.*) They're your people, Gavin. It'll be a chance to find out their wants and needs.

NESBITT. Aye. There'll be a lot of disappointed punters if you don't show your fizzog, Gavvy.

GAVIN CLARK. Oh alright. Wait here. I'll just go and turn off the Mozart.

He goes.

NESBITT. (*Calls.*) There's no need for that! Bring it wi' Yi! Yi can eat it on the way . . .

We see Clark's reaction of discomfiture.

SCENE 12. The pub. Evening.
Andra, Jamesie, Dodie at bar, watching telly, idly. Door opens. Nesbitt enters, with Clark.

NESBITT. Hey, boys! Yeez'll never guess who's here. It's wee Gavvy Clark.

They don't flicker.

ANDRA. (*Gives a half look.*) About time tae. Two lager and a heavy . . .

They each hold up an empty glass, in unison, without turning. Clark reaches for his wallet.

SCENE 13. The pub. Evening.
Much later, they're still at the bar. Clark is relaxed, enjoying himself.

GAVIN CLARK. You know, boys, this evening's done wonders for me! I feel as if I've come home. It's so good to be amongst one's own people again!

ANDRA. Oh, nae bother, Gavvy! One knows whit yi mean, doesn't one, boys?

ALL. Oh aye, one does, one does . . .

GAVIN CLARK. I know, I know, you're joshing me now because I've lost my accent. But believe me, I'm still the same person deep down.

NESBITT. Oh, we believe that awright. (*Draining glass.*) It's your shout again, by the way.

GAVIN CLARK. Of course! Of course! (*Calls.*) Hey, Dougie! (*Attempting Glesga.*) Howk up the swally, pronto, big man! Same again, by the way!

ALL. (*Faking being impressed.*) Hullo! Eh . . . ?

DOUGIE. Allow you, eh Gavin. That old street jive just comes flooding right back, doesn't it, eh?

GAVIN CLARK. Och, don't you start, Dougie! I'm getting enough leg pulling as it is from these characters.

They share a good natured laugh.

Seriously though, guys. It's great to know you've all survived. Especially after all the terrible upheaval that's gone on in Govan this past decade. I suppose the recession must be grim for all of you, eh?

DODIE. Oh aye. Hellish. (*Proffering plate.*) Here, have another smoked salmon sandwich.

GAVIN CLARK. (*Helping himself.*) Don't mind if I do . . .

NESBITT. Tell yeez something though. At least there's wan block in here not complaining. See since the works shut down, Dougie's supplied more red noses than Comic Relief, in't that right, Dougie?

GAVIN CLARK. Aye, it's an ill wind, eh Dougie?

DOUGIE. (*To Gavin.*) Well, you should know. It's blown your arse far enough up the social ladder tae . . .

GAVIN CLARK. Touché, Douglas. (*Laughs it off unconvincingly.*) Well, let's not dwell on the unpleasant aspects of life. This is a reunion, for heaven's sake. Let's enjoy ourselves.

ALL. (*Together, raising glasses.*) Aye!

NESBITT. Aye, fair enough. But I'll need to be getting hame soon. Hey, Dougie, what's the time?

DOUGIE. Thursday.

NESBITT. Christ, is it that late. My tea'll be freezing . . .

Burney enters.

BURNEY. (*To Nesbitt.*) Hey, you. Maw says you've to hurry up. Yir getting finest escalope of veal in a bliddy delicate oriental sauce for your slobber, and it's *freezing*, by the way!

NESBITT. Well, if it's freezing there's nae point hurrying, is there?

Agreement.

(To Clark.) Gavvy, this is my youngest. Meet Burney.

GAVIN CLARK. Hello, Burney, son! My, he's awfie like you, Rab. I think he's going to be tall.

BURNEY. *(To Nesbitt.)* Who's the creep with the brown mooth?

NESBITT. This is Gavvy, son. He's gawn to be the next MP for the area.

BURNEY. Figures. *(To Clark.)* Nae wonder we lost at Culloden . . .

He swaggers off.

NESBITT. *(To Clark.)* See that, eh? That's my boy! That's my boy . . .

DODIE. Aye, he's a credit to yi, Rab. So listen, are we gonny get some serious swallying done or what?

ANDRA. *(Raising glass.)* I'm for getting blootered!

Enthusiastic agreement. Laughs.

GAVIN CLARK. Well, lads, I can't think of anything else I'd rather do. But if you'll excuse me for one minute, I'll just go and ring the wife. Tell her not to wait up!

ALL. Aye, that's the gemme . . .

Clark goes to use the payphone.

DODIE. Allow Gavvy, eh? Husnie changed a bit!

JAMESIE. Deep down he's still one of the boys!

They look, as one, to the payphone.

We see Clark, talking earnestly. He catches them looking, waves, beams a big smile.

ANDRA. *(Through a forced smile.)* Aye, and they've asked me to be the new Conan after Schwartzenager . . .

They wave back, as one, through fixed smiles.

Rat

SCENE 14. Nesbitt's street. Night.
The bunch (Jamesie, Dodie, Nesbitt, Andra, Clark) walking along, fish suppers in hand, towards Nesbitt's house. They're happy.

DODIE. Some night, by the way, boys! Some night, eh . . . !

All enthusiastic agreement.

JAMESIE. Hey, Rab. Are you sure it'll be awright taking a carry out back to your hoose? Will Mary not be annoyed nor nothing?

NESBITT. See you, Cotter. You've always got to put a damper on things, haven't yi! You're nothing' but a wee . . .

ANDRA. (*Restraining him.*) Hey, hey! Easy Rab! Steady the buff!

DODIE. (*Also restraining.*) Aye, Rab, let the buff be steady! (*To Clark.*) Just a wee lovers' tiff, Gavvy boy! Yi enjoying yirself?

GAVIN CLARK. Oh yes, aye. Just like old times, isn't it, eh? (*Looks at his watch, fretfully, muttering.*) Come on . . . Come on . . . !

NESBITT. (*To Clark.*) Yi coming in for a swally, Gavvy son?

GAVIN CLARK. (*Hedging.*) Oh, well I'd uh . . .

Car horn sounds. He looks. The Labour Party van appears, Steven at the wheel.

(*To bunch.*) There's Steven! Wonder what he wants.

GAVIN CLARK. Excuse me a second, won't you lads. (*Hurries over.*)

(*Leaning into the van.*) What the hell kept you? They were starting to get restless. I was nearly swinging my wrist back and forward to try and dazzle them!

STEVEN. I couldn't help it. You were phoning from a pub. I could hardly hear your directions for the noise. Anyway, relax, it was all good PR. They'll tell all their grizzly mates. You've got Westminster in your pocket!

GAVIN CLARK. Yes, the things I do for Socialism . . . hold on, I'll just spray some verbal aniseed around. (*Loudly.*) What's that, Steven? Oh no! (*To bunch.*) Lads, I'm going to have to pass. Would you believe it, they want me to de a pre-election head-to-head for Radio Clyde. What can I say?

ANDRA. You could say, 'Sod Radio Clyde'.

GAVIN CLARK. I'd love to, guys. But don't forget, at the end of the day (*showing a clenched fist*) I'm doing this for Govan, not for me.

ALL. (*Showing clenched fists.*) Aye, right on, Gavvy . . .

GAVIN CLARK. (*Getting into van.*) And remember, lads, on election day, it's Labour! It's Gavin Clark!

DODIE. Gavvy, how could we forget?

SCENE 15. The van. Night.

GAVIN CLARK. (*Crumpling up the chip paper in distaste.*) Now I know how David Attenborough felt when he ate swamp lizard with the pygmies . . .

Chucks paper away. Van drives off.

SCENE 16. The Nesbitts' front door. Night.
The bunch are at Nesbitt's door. Nesbitt is fumbling with his key.

NESBITT. 'Mon, boys. In we go.

ANDRA. Wait a minute, Rab. Are yi sure this is awright noo?

NESBITT. Look, what is this? For the last time, this is my hoose! I'm entitled to bring back anybody I want! Yi think I married an ogre? Yi think she's standing behind there with a rolling pin or something? This is 1989, for Christ's sake!

Door opens. Mary stands.

Hullo, Mary, darling . . .

ALL. Hullo, Mary, hen . . . !

She cleaves Nesbitt with the car exhaust. We hear a loud clanging noise.

NESBITT. (*To others, forcing a smile.*) Yi see that, eh? It's wee surprises like that that keep a marriage alive . . .

He slumps down the wall.

ALL. (*Turning on their heels.*) Cheerio, Mary, hen!

MARY. (*Dragging Nesbitt by the collar.*) In . . . !

Rat

SCENE 17. The pub. Late night.
The television. It shows town hall balcony. Four candidates standing (ie Clark, Hosie, SNP and a token nuisance). The returning officer by them.

ANNOUNCER. And the returning officer is almost ready. So any moment now we should have the result of the Govan South by-election . . .

Jamesie, Andra, Dodie are watching the television. Dougie behind the bar.

DODIE. Hey, you know this democracy's not such a bad thing. At least it gets you a look in on election night, eh Dougie?

DOUGIE. Right. (*Filling glass.*) If I see any ancient Greeks, I'll let them know you approve of their system.

JAMESIE. Aye and tell them thanks for the kebabs as well.

Nesbitt enters. He wears a second bandage.

Hey, here's Rab. Surprise, surprise, Rab . . .

NESBITT. You're treading on thin ice, Cotter . . .

ANDRA. Shush, boys! Look! Here comes the result!

ANNOUNCER. (*On telly.*) And the candidates lining up expectantly . . .

They look.

ANDRA. There's Gavvy, look.

DODIE. Wonder what they talk about while they're waiting, eh?

ANDRA. Ach, probably highbrow stuff. It'll be way above oor heads . . .

SCENE 18. The election balcony. Late night.
The candidates are smiling through gritted teeth.

GAVIN CLARK. (*To SNP candidate.*) I don't know why you bothered turning up, you born-again sheep shagger. I've got the crud in my pocket. You're for a right good licking.

SNP CANDIDATE. Well, you're the man for the job alright. With all the licking practice your tongue's had lately.

ANNOUNCER. (*From offstage.*) And the candidates there, no doubt wishing each other good luck, as the Returning Officer prepares to announce the result.

RETURNING OFFICER. As Returning Officer, I declare the following to be an accurate account of the votes cast. Screaming Lord Nuisance . . .

(*Wave from Nuisance.*)

. . . Nil.

(*Nuisance retreats.*)

Gavin Garmouth Clark . . .

ANNOUNCER. (*From offstage.*) Labour.

RETURNING OFFICER. Seventeen thousand, three hundred and thirty.

(*Big cheer. Confident wave, beam from Clark.*)

James Balloon-McSwaggerty . . .

ANNOUNCER. (*From offstage.*) Scottish Nationalist.

RETURNING OFFICER. Seventeen thousand, three hundred and thirty three!

Bigger cheer. The Nationalist leaps about, giving 'V' signs and making macho groin gesture to Clark. Clark looks dumbfounded.

ANNOUNCER. And the Nationalists modest as ever in victory . . .

SCENE 19. The pub. Late night.
The bunch, as before. They're chuffed. Nesbitt's quiet.

ALL. Hull–ooo . . . !

ANDRA. There y'are, eh! That'll learn the wee swine to take us scruff for granted!

DODIE. Aye, nae bother to us! Hey, wait a minute. That's only three of a difference. There's four of us.

They look up to the telly.

SCENE 20. The balcony. Night.
Balcony, as before. The Nationalist getting his back slapped, hand pumped, etc.

RETURNING OFFICER. And finally, Hugh – Crazy Prices, take a swatch at our stoating discounts – Hosie . . .

ANNOUNCER. Conservative.

RETURNING OFFICER. One.

HOSIE. (*Stepping forward, to audience.*) Cheers Rab! Awrabest! And if you want a wee matching mat for roon the toilet bowl, see me at the General Election! (*Winks.*)

SCENE 21. The pub. Night.
The pub as before. Everybody quiet, looking at Nesbitt.

DODIE. Rab Nesbitt. I never thought I'd see the day . . .

JAMESIE. Aye. You're full of surprises, eh Rab?

NESBITT. I don't know what yeez are talking about! My conscience is clear! I've done nothing at all to feel ashamed aboot! (*Takes a sip of drink. To Dougie.*) Hey, Dougie.

DOUGIE. Aye?

NESBITT. (*Proferring glass.*) Pimp a wee dash of arsenic in there, wid yi?

SCENE 22. The gift shop. Day.
Outside the gift shop. Nesbitt standing. Some caricatures in the window, of 'quaint old characters'. A tin whistle can be heard in the background.

NESBITT. (*To audience.*) Look at that, eh? See that?

We get a look at a caricature. It's of Nesbitt holding his rat.

Quaint old Govan characters, painted by Clatty McCutcheon. That's the trouble with the middle class. They think they can just draw yi in, pat yi on the head and you'll roll ower and let them tickle yi on the belly.

The assistant appears in the window. She waves, smiles at Nesbitt. He waves, smiles back.

(*To audience.*) Well, they're not turning me into a tame rebel that easy. (*Calls through glass to assistant.*) Hey doll! Try pamping this above your fireplace!

He bites the head off the rat, spits it at the window. It sticks. The

Complete the well known saying: 'As happy as pigs in . . .'

assistant screams. He turns to Jamesie, who holds a salmon skeleton by the tail.

NESBITT. (*Going.*) 'Mon, Jamesie . . .

JAMESIE. Right, Rab . . .

They walk a few steps. A man with one leg, one eye, is playing a tin whistle. An alsatian sits beside him.

NESBITT. (*Calls.*) Hey, Clatty! You want to be ashamed of yoursel! You're taking the piss out oor history!

CLATTY. (*Calls back.*) Whit yi talking aboot, Nesbitt? That's what history's for! (*To dog.*) *Kill, Calvin . . . !*

The dog pursues Nesbitt and Jamesie, barking. They try to beat it off with the rat and the fish skeleton.

JAMESIE & NESBITT. (*Beating.*) Get tae! Get tae!

They run off.

Rab C. Nesbitt

EPISODE THREE

Holiday

CAST LIST

FIRST CREDITOR	Martin Black
SECOND CREDITOR	Philip McGrade
ELLA COTTER	Barbara Rafferty
JAMESIE COTTER	Tony Roper
SMALL MAN	Jonathan Watson
MARY NESBITT	Elaine C. Smith
RAB C. NESBITT	Gregor Fisher
GASH	Andrew Fairlie
BURNEY	Eric Cullen
FIRST GIRL	Kate Donnelly
SECOND GIRL	Louise Beattie
ANDY THE COURIER	Paul Coia
MANOLO	Supporting artist

SCENE 1. The Nesbitts' house. Day.
Creditors stand, books in hand.

FIRST CREDITOR. (*Shouts.*) Come out Nesbitt! We know you're in there! (*To second creditor.*) Damn't family. They're more trouble than the rest of the street put together.

SECOND CREDITOR. How much do they owe youse?

FIRST CREDITOR. Six months.

SECOND CREDITOR. Six. Is that all? If I can get it down to six, I'm on the bonus of a solar calculator.

Jamesie and Ella Cotter, walking along. They carry brand name carrier bags. They stop to watch.

ELLA. Would yi not look at that. Sends a shudder right doon yir spine. What a way to live.

JAMESIE. Aye, you're right there, Ella. I'm glad we're respectable noo. (*Calls to Nesbitt's window.*) Gawn yirsel, Rab! Give them the fingers! Stick it right up them! (*to second creditor*) Hey, you'll never take Rab Nesbitt, by the way. He's too fly for the likes of youse.

SECOND CREDITOR. Oh aye? Well we'll see about that. In the Lazy L DIY centre we don't scare easy.

FIRST CREDITOR. (*To Ella, consulting book.*) While we're on the subject, what's your names, by the way?

ELLA. (*Snatching Jamesie back, protectively.*) You'll not find us in there. Yeez've got no hooks in the Cotters. Everything in these bags is bought and paid for. Including wur continental holiday.

JAMESIE. Aye. We're going to Benidorm.

ELLA. (*Nudging him.*) But not the touristy part of Benidorm! No, we're going to the quaint old fishing village part. (*To Jamesie.*) Stumor . . . !

SECOND CREDITOR. Aye, weel I'm sure Benidorm deserves yeez. Now if yeez don't mind, we've got work to do.

A small man in a smart suit appears. He holds a large envelope.

(*To small man.*) Hey, where'd you think you're going?

SMALL MAN. (*Indicating the Nesbitts' house.*) No, you don't understand. I'm just going to . . .

FIRST CREDITOR. Just wait your turn, pal, like the rest of us.

The Nesbitts' window. The curtains flicker. Mary peeps out.

THIRD CREDITOR. Look boys! There she is!

ALL. Nesbitt! Nesbitt!

Mary's face, aghast at window. Curtains shut, hastily.

SCENE 2. The Nesbitts' living room. Day.
Mary at the window. Nesbitt seated, reading paper. Gash and Burney present.

MARY. (*At window.*) Rab! They've spotted us! For God's sake will you do something!

NESBITT. Aye, awright, awright. How close are they?

Mary peeks out from behind the curtains. A face looms up.

MARY. Bliddy close!

GASH. (*Hovering, expectantly.*) Is it time, Da?! Is it time?!

NESBITT. (*Rising.*) Aye, son. Bring me out Big Betsy!

GASH. (*Opening cupboard.*) Hull-oo . . . !

NESBITT. Burney, son. Brek out the ammo!

BURNEY. (*Raking through a drawer.*) Right, Da!

SCENE 3. The Nesbitts' house. Day.
The creditors gathered at the door, banging.

FIRST CREDITOR. (*Shouting.*) Nesbitt! This is Comfydown Soft Furnishings! Give us back our sleep centre!

A window is opened above. Nesbitt leans out, aiming an air rifle.

NESBITT. I'll give you sleep centre awright. It'll be the big sleep for you, boy!

He fires. A pellet shatters a car wing mirror. The creditors dive for cover.

SECOND CREDITOR. You're mad, you people! Completely mad! (*Another shot shatters a windscreen.*) (*To others.*) Christ, let's beat it!

Rab C. Nesbitt

This is worse than the Alamo . . .

Burney at the upstairs window, holding out a smouldering cover.

BURNEY. (*Waving it about.*) Burn, duvet, burn . . . !

Mary emerges beside him. Skites him.

MARY. (*Skitting.*) Ya stupid wee messin yi! That was bought and paid for!

BURNEY. Aya! Sorry maw. I thought we just owned the vallance . . .

SCENE 4. Street. Day.
A car vanishes up the street. Creditors hanging from the doors.

SCENE 5. The Nesbitts' living room. Day.
Nesbitt blows imaginary smoke from the barrel of his rifle. Gash reloads his pistol, excitedly.

GASH. I got one in the ass, Da, and I think I winged a filofax!

NESBITT. Good boy, that's the gemme, that's the gemme . . .

GASH. (*Looking out.*) D'yi think they'll be back?

NESBITT. They might, son. They'll maybes wait to nightfall, then rush us with a court order. But we'll be ready for them wuln't we!

GASH. Bliddy right! See me, Da, at times I love being poor. There's nothing like it for zapping up the adrenalin!

NESBITT. (*Tousles Gash's hair.*) Gash boy, there's hope for you yet. In't there, Mary? I'm saying, in't there?

They hug, laugh. Mary's sitting, sobbing, clutching her blackened duvet.

NESBITT. (*Crossing to her.*) Mary, hen, Mary, what's the matter?

MARY. Don't touch me, Rab Nesbitt! I'm sick of you! I'm sick of living this way! Look at my good duvet. I smoked like a bliddy beagle in a laboratory to save up enough coupons for that. It's aye the same. All wur lives we've had nothing. Everything turns to ashes in wur hands. I'm sick of it!

NESBITT. Och come on, Mary, hen, look on the bright side.

MARY. What bright side?

NESBITT. At least we've still got each other.

MARY. (*Pulling away.*) Don't rub it in.

Door bursts open. Burney enters, driving the small man before him with a garden fork.

BURNEY. Look, Da! I found another one, trying to sneak in past the burnt settee in the back green!

SMALL MAN. No, honestly! You've got the wrong idea! I don't want to take anything from you, I want to give you something.

NESBITT. Aye, and I'll give you something. Gash, hand me my tomahawk!

GASH. (*Doing so.*) Right, Da!

SMALL MAN. No, honestly, it's true, look!

He holds out a piece of paper. Nesbitt snatches it, reads.

NESBITT. Gie's the bliddy thing. (*Reads.*) Holiday to Ken. Who the hell's Ken?

SMALL MAN. No, it says holiday token! Token! Look, (*Points.*) 'Congratulations on winning our expenses paid holiday for four in Benidorm. Thank you for buying our oven chips.'

MARY. Oven chips? God, and I only bought them to flirt with the age of techno culture.

SMALL MAN. Well it's paid off, Mrs Nesbitt. Because you're a winner!

MARY. Me? A winner?

NESBITT. Did yeez hear that, boys. We've won a holiday! We've won a bliddy holiday!

GASH & BURNEY. Hull-oo . . . !

NESBITT. Nae bother to us, eh! (*Frowns, to small man.*) Hey, pal. There's just one thing though.

SMALL MAN. Yes?

NESBITT. What is a holiday, by the way?

Lord and Lady Giro make their way to the VIP departure lounge.

SCENE 5. Airport. Day.
Glasgow Airport.

Holidayish music.

Taxi pulls up. The Nesbitt family get out, struggling with bags, etc. They're dressed in holiday mood. Nesbitt emerges last. Looks about, blinking.

MARY. What's the matter with you?

NESBITT. Nothing. It's just this is the first time I've ever got out of a motor without having a blanket over my heid, that's all.

MARY. (*Yanking him.*) Come on . . . hurry up! We don't want to be late!

SCENE 6. Airport lounge. Day.
Some travellers standing, waiting. Jamesie and Ella among them.

JAMESIE. (*Beaming to all and sundry.*) Three-hour delay. That's brilliant, eh! It'll give us all time to play on the escalators and watch the erries coming in and that!

ELLA. (*Clips him.*) Will you chuck it! For Christ's sake act miserable. We don't want people to think we've never been abroad before. (*Consults watch, tut-tuts.*)

JAMESIE. I don't care. I'm lapping this up. In fact, see, if only my mate Rab was here, my whole life would be complete.

Nesbitt and family appear, hurrying into view.

NESBITT. (*From afar. Waving voucher.*) Jamesie! Jamesie! We've won a holiday! We've won a holiday!

JAMESIE. (*Arms outstretched, looking skyward.*) Cheers, God. Now if you could just do something about the damp in wur scullery . . .

Nesbitt rushes up, punches Jamesie in the arm.

NESBITT. Jamesie!

JAMESIE. (*Punching him back.*) Rab!

BOTH. (*Hugging.*) Hulloo!

ELLA. (*To Mary, wearily.*) Dear Christ, eh. The highlight of working class culture. See Benidorm and die.

MARY. I know. All the same, it's still pure brand new, in't it!

ELLA. (*With a reluctant smile.*) I know!

Gash and Burney have spotted two girls of about their own age.

BURNEY. (*To Gash.*) See what I see?

GASH. Aye . . .

BURNEY. 'Mon . . .

They approach the girls.

BURNEY. Morning, dolls. Allow us for to introduce wurselves. My name's Burney. This is my brother Gash.

GASH. Hi there . . .

BURNEY. Afore we go, there's one thing you should know about us. I like my bacon crispy in the mornings and he likes his rare. Got me? See yeez in Spain . . .

GASH. Buona Sera, by the way . . .

They swagger off. First Girl is about to shout something after them. Second Girl claps a hand over her mouth, preventing her.

Right: As a seasoned traveller I'm blase about jet setting.
Left: We're men of few words – do yeez drop them or what?

SECOND GIRL. (*To First Girl.*) No, don't bomb them out yet. The waiters might be pigs.

Airport announcer's voice sounds over tannoy.

ANNOUNCER. Passenger announcement. Flight 312 for Benidorm is now boarding at gate 6 (etc.) . . .

JAMESIE. (*To Nesbitt, gravely.*) This is it then, Rab. One small step for man. One giant leap for the B1 culture . . .

They look towards the light, grandly.

SCENE 7. Inside plane after take-off. Day.
Singing is heard over the image of the plane. Raucous voices singing 'Viva Espana'. We hear the stewardess over the intercom say . . .

STEWARDESS VOICE. (*Very refined.*) Would passengers please refrain from stamping their feet, sleeping in the luggage racks and goosing the stewardesses . . . (*Little yell, Glesga.*) Hey, get your paws off the goods, pal . . .

SCENE 8. Airport abroad. Evening.
Passengers are disembarking. All drunk. Nesbitt emerges, supported by Jamesie and Mary.

JAMESIE. (*To stewardess, supporting Nesbitt.*) It's awright, doll. Just that wee spot of turbulence. It wasnae the bevvy, honest . . .

NESBITT. No, it wisnae the bevvy. Where's the grun, by the way, doll? Where'd they keep the grun in Spain?

JAMESIE. It's under your feet, Rab. Same as at hame.

NESBITT. Thank Christ for that.

He stoops, prostrates himself, kisses the tarmac.

ELLA. (*To Jamesie.*) See that. I wisht I put as much passion into it when you were kissing me.

JAMESIE. Be fair, Ella. At least the tarmac's warm.

The two girls emerge. First Girl looks queasy and is covering her mouth. Burney approaches her.

BURNEY. (*To First Girl.*) Got a wee touch of the boak, eh doll? Here, you can have a lend of my sick bag if you want. (*She takes it, opens it.*) It's only half full . . .

She turns away and is sick. Burney regards her for a moment.

BURNEY. (*To Second Girl as First Girl is sick.*) Tell her if it's any consolation, this is me seeing her at her worst. And I'd still give her one, okay.

SECOND GIRL. She'll be glad to know her living's not been in vain.

BURNEY. *Ciou.*

The name's Rab C. Nesbitt, pal. But since I'm on holiday I'm dropping the 'C' for the fortnight, just to be informal.

SCENE 9. Airport customs hall. Evening.
Nesbitt approaches passport control. Slides over passport.

NESBITT. (*To officer.*) Awright there, Senora? El Tel, eh? Hasta la vista, and that, eh?

Officer studies passport.

NESBITT. (*To officer.*) It's Rab C. Nesbitt, by the way. Only I'm dropping the 'C' for a fortnight to be informal. (*Brief spasm of dancing.*) This is us on wur holidays, know! Eh, Senor?

Cold look from officer.

NESBITT. (*To audience.*) That's the thing about contempt, eh? Knows no bounderies. (*To family.*) 'Mon youse . . .

SCENE 10. Hotel foyer. Evening.
The new residents assembled.

ANDY. Well, ladies and gentlemen, welcome to Spain. My name's Andy. I'll be your courier for the duration of your stay.

ELLA. (*To Mary.*) He's nice, in't he?

MARY. He is that . . .

JAMESIE. (*Leaning in between them.*) Probably an El Homo if you ask me . . .

Ella elbows him.

ANDY. No doubt you're all tired after the long delays, so I'll let you get off to your beds. Before you go, I'll answer the two main questions that I know are on all of your lips. The exchange rate's 174 pesetas to the pound. And yes, you can drink the water.

Polite titters. Nesbitt mutters to himself, frowning.

ANDY. What's the matter, Mr Nesbitt. Didn't you understand about the money?

NESBITT. No, no, I know about the money awright. I was just wondering what the hell water was?

Laughter.

NESBITT. (*To audience.*) Just a wee bit of role playing, know? Lets everybody know who the character is, din't it?

Porter appears.

ANDY. Now please follow Manolo and he'll show you to your rooms. Goodnight, everyone.

ALL. Goodnight . . .

ANDY. Goodnight, *Andy*!

ALL. Goodnight, Andy . . . !

BURNEY. Sod off, Andy . . .

MARY. (*Clipping him.*) That's enough of that you. Don't forget, we're abroad noo. We're ambassadors for Govan.

NESBITT. (*Clipping Gash.*) At's right. This is where the posh bit starts. So we don't want youse giving us a showing up, in't that right, Mother?

MARY. That's right. Let's show them we Scots've got class. Awright?

GASH AND BURNEY. Awright . . .

Rab C. Nesbitt

SCENE 11. Hotel room. Evening.
Manolo opens the door.

MANOLO. Your room, sir.

MARY AND NESBITT. (*Brushing past him, big roar.*) Hull-ooo . . . !

Nesbitt takes a flier onto the bed, starts bouncing up and down.

MARY. (*Remembering dignity, proferring coin.*) Thank you. (*To Nesbitt.*) Oh Rab, would you look at all this. In't this not the last word in class and sophistication, by the way?

NESBITT. You're not kidding. Listen. It's got the wall to wall music and everything.

MARY. I think that's more the disco under the flerr, actually.

We get a look at her feet. The floorboards vibrating beneath them.

MARY. Now come off that bed till I get a look at the mattress . . .

NESBITT. (*Getting off.*) Ach, who cares about the mattress, Mary? We're in Spain! (*Hugs her.*) Who'd have thought we'd see the day when trash like us would be buying stuff like flip-flops and insect repellant? (*Holds some up.*)

MARY. (*Laughs.*) Aye, you're right! Just think. Two weeks, all to wurselves. A once in a lifetime chance to deepen wur relationship. And to discover the hidden Rab and Mary Nesbitt.

NESBITT. Aye, that's the gemme, eh.

Door opens, Jamesie enters. He looks eager.

JAMESIE. Hey, Rab, that's me ready. You coming for some of that continental swally or what?

NESBITT. Aye, a wee minute, Jamesie. I'll just get cleaned up.

He removes a cigarette from behind his ear, peels off a grubby elastoplast.

NESBITT. Okay, that's me! (*To Mary.*) While I'm away, you start looking for the hidden you. The hidden me's a wee tate easier to find. So this'll gie you time to get a heid start. Awright, Jamesie!

JAMESIE. Awright, Rab, boy!

They go.

MARY. (*Tossing down a magazine.*) It's my own fault. I keep on buying that Cosmopolitan. And I swally it every time . . .

She heaves a suitcase onto the bed with a grunt.

SCENE 12. Hotel bar. Evening.
Entrance to hotel bar.

Nesbitt and Jamesie pause for a moment.

JAMESIE. Listen, we'll just have a couple, eh. I mean we don't want to get blootered on the first night, do we?

NESBITT. No, no. We'll just have one or two as a nightcap, right.

SCENE 13. Bus. Morning.
On board a coach, driving along. Close up on Andy, beaming.

ANDY. (*Through a mike.*) Good morning, everybody! Are we all bright-eyed and bushy-tailed?

ALL. Yes, Andy!

Nesbitt and Jamesie sitting together, asleep, blootered-looking.

ANDY. Well perhaps not quite all of us. Well today we're taking a journey of enchantment and discovery around the old town. And if you look to your left you'll see the quaint old fisherman's disco and wine bar. While over on the right . . .

Mary and Ella sitting together while Andy continues. Ella leans over and nips Jamesie viciously on the ear. He moans in his sleep.

ELLA. (*To Mary.*) I love doing that, so I do. I canny honestly say I like men, do you?

MARY. I canny say I've ever really thought about it.

ELLA. You should. See me, I think about nothing else. See that. That's been a millstone round my neck all my life.

JAMESIE. (*Smiling, half asleep.*) Awright, Ella, sweetheart?

ELLA. Curl up and die! (*To Mary.*) You know the only men I've ever admired apart from Red Adair and King Solomon?

MARY. Who?

ELLA. Butchers! Often I hang around the cutting blocks in their shops hoping to hear them keen the edge of their blades on the grinders.

MARY. What'd you do that for?

Ella looks at Jamesie. We see him spread his legs in his sleep. Ella looks back at Mary.

ELLA. (*Wipes away dribble of saliva.*) Wishful thinking I suppose. What about you. What is it you want from Rab?

MARY. (*Looks at him.*) Consciousness would be a start . . .

Gash and Burney seated. The two girls behind them. They're turned, talking to them.

GASH. I'm just saying to my Br'ar here. That's the great thing about holidays. You do things you widnae normally do at hame, know?

Excuse me, I'm from the social security. How come you can afford this holiday?

GIRL. Oh aye? And what have you done that you widnae do at home? Apart from walk across the carpet without getting chips stuck to your feet.

GASH. (*Attempts a laugh.*) I like you! You're got spirit! (*Turns to Burney.*) Sarky cow . . .

ANDY. Well everyone, that concludes our trip. You've discovered the town, and it's a lovely day, so I expect lots of you will be wanting to discover the beach now, eh?

ALL. Yes.

(*Andy encouraging them.*) Yes, *Andy!*

ANDY. That's the game!

The passengers begin to get off the bus.

BURNEY. (*To Andy.*) Hey, pal. Can I ask you a question?

ANDY. What?

GASH. Are you for real or what?

ANDY. (*Ruffles his hair, laughs.*) Sod off, ya wee hun, or I'll rip your bliddy face off! (*Resumes laughing.*) See you all at dinner!

GASH. (*To Burney.*) See. Telt yi he was normal.

SCENE 14. Beach. Day.
Nesbitt in deck chair. Mary struggling to put hers up. Gash and Burney ogling. A beach trader hurries up to Nesbitt.

TRADER. (*Proffering.*) Melon! Melon!

NESBITT. (*Drawing back a hand.*) Who're you calling a melon? Get to!

A topless girl walks past. Gash and Burney express admiration. Mary skites them.

MARY. (*Skiting.*) Cut that out youse!

GASH AND BURNEY. Aya!

MARY. Anybody's think you'd never seen a lassie before! There's nothing wrang with the human body! It's a perfectly normal, natural and healthy thing!

GASH. Does that mean you're going to go topless then, Maw?

MARY. Certainly not. I think it's disgusting.

BURNEY. Thank Christ for that.

NESBITT. (*Skitting him.*) Shuttit you! And don't be a sexist! Your Maw's got great tits!

MARY. (*Mortified, sits.*) Louder, Rab. I think somebody in Kirkcaldy missed that. (*Removes her cardigan, shudders.*) Oh would you just feel that sun! It fair caresses yi like a lover's finger tips, by the way. Rab, darling. Would you not like to slide your deckie up a wee tate closer?

NESBITT. (*Rising.*) Nah, bugger that. I'm sliding nothing up naewhere. I think I'll just take a donner about. See if I can hunt down a yesterday's Daily Record.

MARY. Thank you, Julio Inglasias. (*To Gash and Burney.*) What about youse, boys? You coming to sit by your mammy?

BURNEY. Yi kidding? It's somebody to sit on wur coupon we want. (*To Gash.*) 'Mon . . .

GASH. (*Shielding his eyes, notices something.*) Haw, Maw. Can yi get snow blindness in the Costa Blanco?

MARY. Don't be daft! How?

GASH. (*As they go.*) Just wondered . . .

Jamesie appears by Mary. He wears a skimpy thong. His body is very white. He clutches a bottle of coconut oil. Ella spreads a towel on the sand.

JAMESIE. (*Liberally dowsing himself.*) In't this not the gemme, Mary, hen? This is what I call living!

ELLA. You watch yourself with that stuff. You know what they said about overdoing it on the first day.

JAMESIE. Ach, rubbish! (*Still sluicing.*) Listen, woman, I've worked on building sites in the blazing heat of Paisley! I've toiled in the scuderoony under my boiler suit at the Parkhead Forge! Hell holds no surprises for Jamesie Cotter! (*Shouting at the sun.*) So come on, ya durty big yella beauty yi! Do your worst!

He spreadeagles himself on the towel.

JAMESIE. Ea-sy . . . !

ELLA. (*To Mary.*) I know. Like the Charge of the Light Brigade, wasn't it? Magnificent, but futile . . .

They look down at him.

JAMESIE. (*Spreadeagled.*) Hull-oo . . . !

SCENE 15. Street. Day.
Meanwhile Nesbitt is walking along a shopping street.

NESBITT. (*To audience.*) Tell yi one thing though. For a block like me, it takes a bit of getting used to this. Scum in the sun. I've never seen this much daylight. In fact the nearest I ever get to a sun tan is when the police shine a torch on me when I'm lying in the close on a Saturday night.

A girl in a bikini walks past.

NESBITT. And nookie. Thurs a lot of nookie in the air. In the West of Scotland we don't actually have sex. We just stand in wur underwear and throw chips at each other across the floor. My weans were actually conceived from a bit of bacteria on a mutton pie. All the same, I widnae mind getting in the holiday mood. (*Stops a young man who's dressed in trendy summer gear.*) (*To man.*) Hey, Jim. Where'd yi get your gear, by the way? I lap it up! It's pure gallus, so it is!

YOUNG MAN. (*Foreign accent.*) Lap it up? Gallus?

NESBITT. (*Demonstrating.*) Troosers, by the way! Pantaloni!

YOUNG MAN. Ah, pantaloni! There. (*Points to shop.*)

NESBITT. Cheers! Awrabest! (*To audience.*) See me? I'm for a wee dod of that by the way.

He hurries into the shop.

SCENE 16. Street. Day.
Nesbitt hurries out of shop.

He's dressed as before but for a pair of loud floral Bermuda shorts and gleaming white trainers. He carries his old clothes under his arm in a brown paper parcel.

NESBITT. (*Modelling.*) See that, eh? Look at that! This is the real me coming oot noo. Under all the soot and the chip fat and that. I'm like Glesga, boy! I've been sartorially sandblasted. Know the trouble with us British? We're too reserved. Too timid. Too shy, know? (*Shouts at passing stranger.*) Haw! Haw, Pedro! Where'd I get a Daily Record roon here?

Puzzled look from stranger.

Dailyo Recordo! You know, moaning-faced Scottish rag!

STRANGER. (*Foreign accent.*) Ah, moaning-faced Scottish rag! (*Points to shop.*)

NESBITT. Cheers, pal. Awrabest! Gibralter and that! Viva Franco! (*To audience.*) They're dead chuffed if you try and learn the lingo.

The stranger spits on the ground, goes.

Of course, I huvnie quite cracked the accent yet . . .

Goes.

SCENE 17. Street. Day.
Gash and Burney standing, chatting to the two girls.

GASH. (*To First Girl.*) It's magic being abroad, in't it. For once in your life you feel normal. Instead of being Scottish.

FIRST GIRL. I know what you mean. But I'm determined not to enjoy it too much. Coz I'll just feel all the more miserable when I get back.

GASH. Aye. It takes keech to unnerstan keech, so it does? (*They hold hands.*)

SECOND GIRL. (*To Burney.*) Tell yi one thing about Spain though. They've no idea of style, have they. Look at the state of that yin, lowping down the street . . .

They all look at the person who's lowping. It's Nesbitt.

NESBITT. (*Calling from afar.*) Hullo there, boys! Yeez awright?

GASH AND BURNEY. (*Together, mortified.*) Oh, no . . .

FIRST GIRL. (*As the girls go.*) See you around then, eh Gash . . . ?

GASH. (*To Burney.*) Look at that, eh? Three hours of my best sincerity, blown in half a second.

A rolled up Daily Record wallops both over the head.

NESBITT. (*Hugging them.*) That was me away getting my paper. (*Beaming.*) Did yeez miss me?

They look at him.

SCENE 18. Beach. Day.
Two ambulancemen are around Jamesie, lifting him onto a stretcher. Jamesie moans, agonised. Mary and Ella stoop over him.

JAMESIE. (*Getting loaded onto stretcher.*) Aaah, watch my back, senor! El backo, aahh . . . (*Imploringly.*) Ella! Ella! I'm in agony!

ELLA. I'm not exactly basking in this myself. Could yi not keep your screaming down. I don't want the whole beach to know I married a stumor.

JAMESIE. You're a hard wumman, Ella Cotter. I'll tell yi one thing though. This is the nearest I've came to having a hot flush since I married you!

Ella's eyes narrow. She moves in on him.

JAMESIE. No! No!

Ella draws her fingernails slowly down Jamesie's front. Jamesie howls.

MARY. Och come on, Ella. That was a bit much.

ELLA. Och, so what. He's a man, in't it. That'll gie him a glimmer of how a caeserian feels.

Jamesie is borne away. Nesbitt stops him.

NESBITT. (*Slapping him, with paper.*) Awright there, Jamesie? (*Jamesie howls.*) (*To Ella.*) He looks a bit rough. You better just keep him to the beer this afternoon.

They look toward Jamesie. We see, from their point of view the beach trader hurry up to Jamesie.

TRADER. (*Proffering.*) Melona! Melona!

JAMESIE. . . . . off!

SCENE 19. Gash and Burney's hotel room. Day.
Gash is standing by the window, dressing. Mary is tidying up the room. Burney lies on the bed, reading.

MARY. (*Tidying, to Burney.*) Shift your feet. (*To Gash.*) What are you getting all titivated up for? Is that you going oot with that lassie again?

BURNEY. Call that a lassie? That's for six month in quarantine when we get back.

MARY. (*Skites him.*) Shuttit you! At least he's got some romance in his disposition!

GASH. (*Buttoning his shirt at window.*) Aye, you're right there, Maw. For once in my life there's magic in the air. And not only magic. Look at that . . .

Mary joins him at the window.

GASH. Who says miracles don't happen? It's even snowing on the Costa Brava.

They look out. Snowflakes fall.

MARY. In the name a God . . .

At the same time Jamesie and Ella on veranda. Ella is brushing Jamesie's bare skin. He moans, gently, as snowflakes of skin drift downwards.

We see Mary and Gash at the window with Jamesie and Ella above.

Music. Something nocturnally romantic.

SCENE 20. Tourist street. Night.
Shops. Pubs. People sitting, drinking.

Nesbitt walks by, eating a fish supper.

NESBITT. (*To audience.*) Tell yi one thing, boy. It's a wonderful world and no mistake! Have yeez seen it? Here, go ahead, take a swatch. Be my guest, look. It's got the stars, the grun, the whole works. And I'll tell yi, see when you look close, it's a helluva colour scheme too. See how the sky just matches the water there. Ye canny buy that. Some interior decorator, God, by the way. In fact, see me, I'm glad I bought new shoes coz it's a privelege to walk in this world sometimes. In fact, see the only thing that spoils it . . . (*He stops by a noisy pub. People at outside tables, being loud.*) (*Indicating.*) . . . Shite like me. Look at them. Sitting there with their big baw faces and their arteries full of Cookeen, trying to kid on the waiters that they're playboys. (*Shouting at them.*)

Scum in the sun!

You're not playboys! You're not playboys! You're just trash in new kaks, same as me!

Noises of animal protest.

NESBITT. (*Moving on.*) Ach, gawn! Get to! (*To audience.*) Tell yi wan thing. I'm glad I'm miserable. Life's not buying off Rab C. Nesbitt with the Birdy song and a dose of skitters. I'll walk alone, boy! And I'll tell yi another thing. Universe is it? Harmony is it? (*Points up.*) See that durty big swine up there, by the way? That big pock-faced man in the moon there?

There is a full moon.

I'm gonny wipe the smile off that yin's coupon afore my time's up on this earth, boy. Hanging about there with a durty big grin on its fizzer, making oot it knows everything. Well it knows *nothing*, boy! It knows *nothing*! It's just a durty big lump of keech staggering around in circles, same as me! (*Walking on.*)

Ach, but what am I telling youse for? Youse don't know what I'm talking about. Naebody knows what I'm talking aboot . . .

He stops. A second, foreign Nesbitt, identically dressed, is shouting at the moon, shaking his fist. The foreign Nesbitt stops shouting. The two Nesbitts regard each other. The foreign Nesbitt points to his bandage.

FOREIGN NESBITT. Bandage! Bandage!

NESBITT. Aye, bandage, pal. That's the gemme. You tae, eh?

FOREIGN NESBITT. (*Embracing Nesbitt.*) Mon frere!

NESBITT. (*To audience.*) There y'are, eh? There's nothing that restores your faith in human nature more than meeting some other poor bastard that's as mad as yourself. (*Going.*) Awrabest, Pedro!

He walks on. Gash and First Girl appear, hand in hand.

NESBITT. Hullorerr, doll. Yi awright?

FIRST GIRL. Aye, fine, Mr Nesbitt. Gash and me are just having a wee walk in the moonlight.

GASH. (*Bashful.*) I'll try not to be too late back, Da.

NESBITT. That's awright, son. You take all the time in the world. (*To audience.*) He disnae realise it yet. But it's all doonhill from there. (*Drawing back hand to cuff the moon.*) Get to . . . !

SCENE 21. Tourist gift shop. Day.
Tourists milling about. Nesbitt looking at some items of junk. Mary at the counter, attempting to get served. The assistant ignores her, serving other tourists with more expensive items.

NESBITT. (*To audience.*) Some amount of keech in the world, in't there, eh? No matter where yi go dosh rules though, eh. Seen this? Take a swatch at this.

MARY. (*At counter holding up small item, timidly.*) Eh, excuse me, do you think I could have this wee . . .

ASSISTANT. (*Brushing her aside.*) One moment . . .

NESBITT. See that, eh? That's the working class all ower. If we're not rampaging about, eating the El Greco's, we're sliding along the walls, like wee mice, scared to talk above a squeak. (*To Mary.*) What's the matter, Mary, hen?

Holiday

MARY. I'm trying to buy this wee matador for my Mammy. But these big Americans keep pushing in front of me.

NESBITT. I see, I see. (*Taps American tourist on shoulder.*) Hey, Jim. Excuse me, by the way.

AMERICAN. Pardon me, are you Scottish? My wife and I just love Scotland.

NESBITT. Oh good, good . . . (*To audience.*) Some boys the yanks, eh? I've not been patronised this much since the Queen opened the drying oot ward in the Southern General.

AMERICAN. I suppose you must have your own tartan. What is your name, by the way?

NESBITT. No, I don't have a tartan. And my name's Rab. But you can call me Dunk.

AMERICAN. Why do they call you Dunk?

NESBITT. Listen . . . (*He nuts the American. We hear a 'dunk' noise.*) On you go, Mary hen . . .

MARY. (*To assistant.*) Hey, you. Pamp that in a poke, pronto. And nane of your lip, or you'll get the bliddy same. (*To Nesbitt.*) How was that, Rab? Was that okay?

NESBITT. Nae bother, hen. Spoke like a native.

Winks to audience.

SCENE 22. On board coach. Morning.
Mary and Ella sitting together, asleep, post blootered. Nesbitt and Jamesie together. Andy, bright, fresh.

ANDY. Good morning everyone!

ALL. Good morning Andy!

ANDY. And are we all bright-eyed and bushy-tailed this morning?

JAMESIE. (*To Nesbitt.*) See if he says that one more time, I'm gonny punch his bliddy lights oot.

ANDY. (*To Jamesie.*) And what's wrong with your good ladies this morning. A wee touch too much Sangria perhaps?

JAMESIE. Sangria, bollocks. They'd to get blootered on Carly

Specials to dodge listening to your crummy patter!

NESBITT. Easy, Jamesie, easy. (*To Andy.*) No offence, pal. He's just upset coz it's wur last day, know?

ANDY. I see . . .

NESBITT. All the same, your patter is humming. And I mean that in a constructive way. (*To Jamesie.*) Never mind, Jamesie. Seeing as it's wur last night, we'll go pure mental the night. We'll do something crazy, that we've never done afore.

JAMESIE. What, Rab?

NESBITT. We'll stay sober.

JAMESIE. Sobriety, eh! I've heard about that. But I've never had the nerve to try it. Och, bugger it, what am I holding back for at my age? I'll do anything for kicks! Count me in, Rab. You're on!

NESBITT. That's the gemme, Jamesie!

JAMESIE. Only one thing, Rab. Keep it schtum for noo, eh? I mean we don't want the lassies thinking we've turned degenerate.

They look at the women. They sleep, mouths agape, black eyed, horrible.

JAMESIE AND NESBITT. (*Together, punching each other.*) Hull-ooo . . . !

SCENE 23. Beach. Night.
Frollicking noises from the sea.

Nesbitt and Ella, Jamesie and Mary rush out, all holding hands.

ALL. (*Rushing out.*) Hull-ooo . . . !

They fall to the sand, in 'From Here To Eternity' style.

JAMESIE. I'll tell yi something, Mary, hen. This is the drunkest I've felt in years. And I huvnie even touched a drop!

MARY. Me neither! If I could buy this high at Viccy wines, I'd have a half bottle in my message bag every day!

JAMESIE. You know something, Mary. I've never telt you this. But see you. You're a fine looking wumman, by the way.

MARY. And you're . . . a fine looking man, Jamesie.

They touch each other's arms, lightly.

Nesbitt, next to them, watching, taken aback.

NESBITT. In the name a Christ . . . (*Turns to Ella.*) Hey Ella. This is the most jaked I've felt in years, and I huvnie even had a swally yet.

ELLA. Aye. It is quite pleasant, in't it?

NESBITT. I've never telt you this. But see you, Ella Cotter. (*Touching her arm.*) You're a fine looking wumman, by the way.

ELLA. And I've never telt you this, Rab Nesbitt. But see you, you're an ugly looking bastard. (*Slapping him.*) And if you don't get your mitts offa me, I'll skewer your tackle with my manicure set!

NESBITT. Oh, I see! It's like that, is it? It's like that. (*To Jamesie.*) Hey, Burt Lancaster!

JAMESIE. Whit?

NESBITT. If I'm not getting yours, you're not getting mine's.

He punches Jamesie, meatily, in the face.

JAMESIE. Aya!

A fight breaks out.

SCENE 24. Beach. Night.
Long shot of the fight. In the forefront of the picture, Burney and Second Girl pop up from the sand.

SECOND GIRL. What's that noise, Burney? Is that somebody coming?

BURNEY. Nah, you're awright. Somebody coming doesn't sound like that. Somebody coming sounds like this . . .

He sighs, deeply.

SCENE 25. Glasgow Airport. Day.
Passengers disembarking from plane. Jamesie and Ella, Mary, Gash and Burney, and First and Second Girls gather at the foot of the stairs.

GASH. (*To First Girl tearfully.*) I'm not going to forget yi. I'll write every day. I'm gonny go straight oot and get 'True Love' tattooed on my knuckles.

Rab C. Nesbitt

This is one of these photos yi look back on in fifteen years saying 'Aye he's deid noo, she had a breast off, he's an alky, she emigrated to Canada . . . '

FIRST GIRL. And I'll never forget you either, Gash!

They kiss, passionately.

Burney watching them. He turns to Girl 2, who waits, expectantly.

BURNEY. (*To Second Girl.*) Well cheers then, doll. I'll gie yi a phone sometime . . . (*Walks off.*)

The creditors appear at the foot of the gangway steps. They stop Jamesie.

FIRST CREDITOR. Where's Nesbitt? Have you seen Nesbitt?

JAMESIE. (*Removes dark glasses to reveal two black eyes.*) Are you kidding? I canny see the heid on top of a pint just now.

ELLA. (*Leading him.*) This way, Jamesie . . .

FIRST CREDITOR. (*To others.*) We'll wait for him. He must be here somewhere.

Holiday

SCENE 26. Glasgow Airport. Day.
*Emergency exit of plane. Nesbitt slides down the chute. The creditors
turn, spot him.*

SECOND CREDITOR. There he is! Get him!

NESBITT. (*To audience.*) That's the thing about gawn on holiday,
in't it. It's nice to get away. But it's good to get back to normal
again, know what I mean? (*Chucking large donkey at them.*) Hasta
la vista, ya bas . . . !

*He gives one finger salute and legs it. They pursue him across the
tarmac.*

Rab C. Nesbitt

EPISODE FOUR

CAST LIST

MARY NESBITT	Elaine C. Smith
DOCTOR	David Troughton
RAB C. NESBITT	Gregor Fisher
NON-SMOKING MAN IN BUS QUEUE	Andrew Dallmeyer
PRIM LADY IN BUS QUEUE	Mary Riggans
BIG MAN IN BUS QUEUE	Martyn James
ANDRA	Brian Pettifer
DODIE	Iain McColl
DOUGIE	Charlie Sim
JAMESIE COTTER	Tony Roper
BURNEY	Eric Cullen
GASH	Andrew Fairlie
VOICE OF PINK ELEPHANT	Russell Hunter
COUNSELLOR	Laurie Ventry
GRAHAM	Norman Lovett
3RD MEMBER OF THERAPY GROUP	Bruce Morton

Drink

SCENE 1. Street. Day.
It's raining heavily.

A queue of women stand waiting for a shop to open. Mary Nesbitt is amongst them. She's smoking. She's laden down with shopping bags and fed up. All the women, including Mary, wear dark glasses.

MARY. (*Noticing audience.*) Oh, it's yirself. Wid yi look at me?

We look at her.

It's on days like these yi feel privileged to be living in the new revitalised Glesga, isn't it? Honest to Christ, they scrape a bit of crap off the sandstone and suddenly we're all supposed to be jumping aboot like sun-drenched Californians or something. Och, I'm sorry to be such a moaning-faced bissom, but it's hard to feel the warm glow of civic pride when you've just spent the last ten minutes picking your totties oot the gutter in the pouring rain coz the honnel's snapped on yir message bag. (*Indicates bag.*) This is the second most popular shop in Govan, by the way, next to the off sales. It's the knicker shop. Where all the women come when they're trying to put a sparkle back into their marriage. Right bunch of bliddy optimists, in't we? And see when yi take a dekko at the critters we've latched on to, yi wonder why we bother. Have yi seen them? Go on, take a swatch across the street. But I'm warning yi, yi'd better stand doonwind or they might catch yir scent and stampede.

We take a swatch across the street.

Jamesie, Dodie, Andra and cronies are greeting each other, drunkenly, as they enter. (Lots of 'see you', 'big man', 'you're magic', etc.)

Mary in queue, watching them.

MARY. (*To audience.*) See what I mean? It's not only the buildings that need renovating roon here, it's the men. Starting from the inside oot. And we're as stupid. Christ, look at us all. (*Removes dark glasses to reveal black eye.*) Not an unmarked set of eyeballs between us and yet we're getting all het up in case the gorillas in the mist have lost that loving feelin. But that's the trouble with being a nestbuilder, you're forever clutching at straws. And let's face it, there's only ever been one mistress roon here and that's drink. The big blond in the pint glass. And I'd like to be able to tell yi that us women had more sense but I've

89

just spotted a Tennant's supercan that musta flew oot my bag when my totties made their break for freedom. Excuse me . . .

She stoops to retrieve the can.

(*Stooping.*) Reduced to this, eh? Plucking things from oot the gutters. (*Frowns.*) That reminds me. Wonder how bozo's getting on at the doctor's . . .

SCENE 2. Doctor's office.
Door opens. Nesbitt pokes his head round, smiling.

DOCTOR. Ah, Mr Nesbitt. Thank you for coming in.

NESBITT. Cheers, boss. Nae bother. Always glad to help oot the National Health and that. Sorry I've not been putting too much business your way. But I've been a bit too bliddy well healthy this eather, know?

DOCTOR. Really. That's not what your X-rays would suggest, I'm afraid.

NESBITT. X-rays? What about my X-rays?

DOCTOR. Sit down, Mr Nesbitt.

Nesbitt sits.

I see your hands are shaking.

NESBITT. I see your nose is running. So what?

DOCTOR. I'll get straight to the point, Mr Nesbitt. How much, approximately, do you drink?

NESBITT. Drink? I've no idea. I'm never sober enough to tally it up, how?

DOCTOR. Let me show you something. (*Rises, points to slide.*) You see that ugly dried up pulp in the shape of a burst slipper here?

NESBITT. Aye.

DOCTOR. That is your liver.

NESBITT. My liver? Can I have a wee swatch at it?

DOCTOR. Please do.

He does.

NESBITT. Allow it, eh? My liver. Imagine that. That wee bugger's been floating aboot inside me for all thae years and I've never yet said as much as 'hullo' to it. (*Tickling slide.*) Ye wee beauty, Yi!

DOCTOR. 'Goodbye' might be a more appropriate word, if you don't start changing your ways.

NESBITT. What'd yi mean? What'd yi mean?

DOCTOR. (*Points.*) You see these spots here?

NESBITT. (*Looks closely.*) Spots? Oh aye . . .

DOCTOR. Those chart the progress of the disease known as cirrhosis.

NESBITT. (*Sits back heavily.*) Cirrhosis?

DOCTOR. Do you know what cirrhosis is?

NESBITT. Of course I know what it is. I'm from the Wine Alley. We only know two long words. 'Cirrhosis' and 'restitution'. What is it you're trying to tell me here, by the way?

DOCTOR. I'm telling you, very simply, that unless you drastically reduce the level of your alcoholic intake, you will be dead within a year.

NESBITT. I see, I see . . . (*Twisting his hands.*) A year, eh? Yi mean like twelve months like?

DOCTOR. That's what I mean.

NESBITT. Tell yi what. Could we not come to a wee arrangement. I'll start taking a wee dash of lime in my Buckfasts, and you add on a wee dod of injury time to my life expectancy kinna style, know?

DOCTOR. You don't understand, Mr Nesbitt. You see, there's nothing that I or anyone else can do to repair the damage you've already done to yourself. So from now on the responsibility for your own life, or death, lies squarely in your own hands.

NESBITT. In my own hands, eh . . . (*Looks at his shaking hands.*) Christ Almighty . . . (*hides them.*) Look Jim, I'll come clean wi' yi. See me, I'm scum, by the way. Bevvy's a way of life to me. I don't know if I can gie it up.

DOCTOR. Then you must take the consequences, Mr Nesbitt.

NESBITT. I wish you'd stop putting the responsibility for my life onto me! That's the trouble with life these days, everybody passes the buck!

DOCTOR. (*Glances at watch.*) Excuse me, I like to get a couple of miles in before lunch.

He rises, strides an exercise bike.

NESBITT. (*Desperate.*) I mean gezza break, Jim. I never asked to be born a waster, did I? I mean with a fizzog like this, could I ever have been anything different?

DOCTOR. Look, try to calm down. I realise this has come as a shock, but you must try to be philosophical. There's more to life than drink, you know.

NESBITT. Not much more, I'll bet. What else is there like?

DOCTOR. Any number of things! Exercise, for one! You must try to take your mind off alcohol.

NESBITT. You're right, no more bevvy. No more bevvy . . .

DOCTOR. That's the stuff. You see, you've had a shock to the system, but you're starting to be rational again.

NESBITT. That's me, boy. Rational's my middle name . . .

DOCTOR. That's the style. Look, you see, your hands have even stopped shaking.

NESBITT. (*Looking.*) Aye, so they have. Tell yi one thing but.

DOCTOR. What's that?

NESBITT. My hands've maybe stopped shaking, but there's not half one helluva puddle under this chair! (*Rises.*)

DOCTOR. Where are you going?

NESBITT. Where the hell d'yi think I'm going after a bit of news like that? I'm going oot to get blootered! (*Looks at his hands. They're shaking again. He slaps them.*) Behave yir bliddy selves . . . !

Storms off. The doctor squints under Nesbitt's chair, registering distaste.

SCENE 3. Street.
Nesbitt exits from the doctor's surgery, walks along street.

NESBITT. What'd yi make of that yin, eh? See that's the trouble with living in Govan. Yi get left with all the numpties that urnie bright enough for the brain drain. Drink too much. Widnae be that if I was a private patient. Oh no. They'd just whap your liver in for a service then fix yi up with a courtesy one to run around with while they scraped the caribuncles off it.

A jogger gets in his way. They perform the universal ritual minuet of blocking each other's path before Nesbitt gets impatient.

Gawn, get tae! Get Tae! (*To audience.*) See thae ginks, thae get right up my onions, so they dae. I mean, what is the matter with people these days. All thae fitness freaks skiting aboot the streets buff naked except for a diver's watch and a set of underwear. Getting all het up if they loss a milli-second through having to mark time at a red light. Make yi bliddy sick just to look at them. I mean, that isnae living is it? I mean, fair enough, I might be a walking pisspot with a penchant for pork scratchings, but it's the quality of life that counts, isn't it? See me, by the way. At heart I'm still a teenager. (*Producing a cigarette.*) Nicotine and caffeine, know what I mean . . .

Stops by a bus queue. Some people in queue carrying sports hold-alls.

(*To man in queue.*) 'Scuse me, Jim, got a light there please?

MAN IN QUEUE. I'm sorry. I don't smoke.

NESBITT. Oh Christ, wan of them . . . (*To queue at large.*) Some of yeez got a light there, by the way?

The queue look at each other.

NESBITT. What, no smokers? Is there nobody normal in this city any more?

A prim looking woman speaks.

WOMAN. Non smoking *is* normal nowadays. It's you that's the odd one.

NESBITT. Aye, you're bliddy right I'm odd. I'm a dying breed me. I *enjoy* myself! I *enjoy* myself! (*Indicating belly to queue.*) See that, by the way, see that . . .

MAN IN QUEUE. We could hardly miss it . . .

NESBITT. Know what this is? A monument to a bygone way of life, that's what that is! When folk got *fun* oot of living. Instead of turning it into a bliddy well endurance race! (*Indicating fat man in queue.*) See him, by the way, see him? He's got the right idea. (*Grabbing man's paunch.*) A big fat bastard. A big roly-poly cheery-faced numpty. (*To man.*) Yi awright there, pal?

FAT MAN. Bugger off.

NESBITT. Ach well, thur an exception to every rule, in't there.

PRIM WOMAN. Look, would you just please go away!

General agreement.

NESBITT. Certainly I'll go away. What'd yeez think. I'm trying to panhandle money for drink or something?

They look at each other.

There y'are, gie a dug a bad name. Coz I'll tell yeez this, I'm off the drink, by the way, I'm not allowed to drink. And I'll tell yeez, this is the best I've felt in years, by the way. I feel magic. I don't miss it! I don't even bliddy well miss it! (*Pause.*) And if yeez believe that, yeez'll believe anything, so get the hons in the pockets pronto, or else I start giving it the Hank Williams. Two, three . . . (*Singing.*) 'Your cheating heart, will tell on you . . .'

Money floods in.

That's the gemme, that's the gemme. I'm self-taught tae, never took a lesson. Cheers, awrabest . . .

The prim woman expresses distaste.

(*To prim woman.*) And I don't know what you're tut-tutting at, by the way. Standing there with a half bottle of voddie keeking oot the handbag!

Nesbitt snatches the vodka bottle, holds it aloft.

Hullo! There y'are, sleekit drinker, by the way! Not like me. At least I'm up front when I fall doon.

The woman grabs the bottle back, mortified.

There y'are, doll. No offence. Hope I huvnie embarrassed yi nor nothing. (*Laughs.*) (*To audience.*) Nice to see the scruff winning one for a change, in't it, eh . . . (*Rattling the money in his hand.*) Easy!

SCENE 4. Pub.
Dougie behind bar.

The cronies, Dodie, Andra, opposite with Nesbitt. Nesbitt is downing a pint. We watch him drain the glass.

ANDRA. And you're not worried then, Rab?

NESBITT. (*Smacks his lips.*) Certainly I'm not worried. See, know my attitude? To me, life's like a party. And it's all a matter of knowing when to leave, know? (*Calls, to Dougie.*) Four heavy, Dougie!

ANDRA. When to leave? Christ, I never even got invited. What aboot you, Dodie?

DODIE. Oh, I got invited awright. (*Frowns.*) It's just that I've always felt there's a better one going on next door, know what I mean?

ANDRA. But the hoose next door to you's boarded up.

DODIE. Aye, I know. And thae winos really know how to swing, believe you me. In fact, see, when I hear them ripping up the floorboards and I get a wee whiff of that Mr Sheen seeping in through the skirting, I often wish I wasnie doomed to be so respectable, know?

NESBITT. Aye, me neither. It's a curse, in't it . . .

DOUGIE. (*Putting up pints.*) Four forty, Nesbitt . . .

NESBITT. Aye, right y'are. (*Producing vast handfuls of change.*) Hope yi don't mind it all in coppers . . .

Glare from Dougie as he begins counting.

And I mean, see when you get right down to it. What's it got to do with anybody else what I do with my life? I mean if I want to drink myself to a standstill that's my affair, in't it?

ANDRA. Spoken like a real man, Rab!

DODIE. A *Govan* man!

ANDRA. Is there any other kind?

ANDRA AND DOUGIE. (*Together, raising glasses.*) Hulloo . . . !

Nesbitt has crossed to a table where Jamesie sits, reading a health leaflet.

NESBITT. (*Proffering him a pint.*) Here, guts, get that doon yir neck.

JAMESIE. I don't want that. Don't you put that on my table.

NESBITT. It's a pint, man. How no'?

JAMESIE. It might be a pint to you. But it's two units of alcohol to me. I've got my waistline to think aboot. Not to mention my insides.

NESBITT. Oh Christ, not another yin. What's brung this on all of a sudden?

JAMESIE. You mean you don't know?

NESBITT. No.

JAMESIE. Well if you don't know, I'm not telling yi.

NESBITT. (*Turning away.*) Suit yirself.

JAMESIE. (*Rising to his feet, pointing.*) I'll tell yi what's brung this on, Rab Nesbitt. Friendship! That's what's brung it on.

NESBITT. What'd yi mean, what'd yi mean?

JAMESIE. Listen, Rab. Me and you go back a long ways the giether, don't we?

NESBITT. We do, we do . . .

JAMESIE. We started going into pubs the gither, didn't we? Then on to Secondary school.

NESBITT. We did, we did that, pal.

JAMESIE. For my twenty-first birthday you gied me heart massage, and ever since then we've followed yi everywhere. (*Putting arms round the others.*) Andra, Dodie . . . the three musketeers, in't that right, boys?

ANDRA. (*Raising glass.*) Here's tae yi, big man!

NESBITT. Aye, very touching. But what's the point, pal, what's the point?

JAMESIE. The point? The point, ya big wet brained slopdredger is that if you're on the way oot with a liver like an insole we must be too. Coz we've matched yi pint for pint, every night, for the last twenty-five bliddy years!

Andra and Dodie, drinking, spray out their beer.

ANDRA. Bastard!

DODIE. (*To Jamesie.*) Who's the stranger?

NESBITT. Oh, I see, I see! I'm getting the blame noo, am I?

JAMESIE. No offence, Rab. But when the great barman in the sky starts getting ready to call last orders, it's every waster for himself. (*Puts down glass.*) Am I right, boys?

ANDRA. Aye. Life's precious, Rab. And I've still got ambitions. I'd hate to have to meet my maker never having managed to grow a decent pair of sideburns, know? (*Puts down glass.*)

DODIE. Andra's right, Rab. It's an expanding universe. Pretty soon there'll be eighteen channels on the telly. Who'd want to die withoot seeing a game show in Flemish! (*Puts down glass.*)

JAMESIE. You see, Rab. There's that much to live for. I mean even you must have some ambitions. Something you'd like to do afore yi . . . shuffle off the old mortal coil.

NESBITT. Aye, there is. But it'll never happen if I live to be a hunner.

JAMESIE. What's that, Rab?

NESBITT. Just once I'd like to talk to you withoot feeling I've just gargled with Preparation X. Gawn, away hame and get yir cocoa . . .

JAMESIE. Aye, well have it your own way then, Rab. (*To others.*) 'Mon, boys. (*To Nesbitt.*) See yi in the cemetary.

NESBITT. (*Calls after them.*) Aye, well you'll need to knock hard on the heidstone! Coz I'll be doonstairs having a ceiledh! (*Mutters.*) Sweetiemooths. (*To Dougie.*) Whit you looking at?

DOUGIE. A nutter. A mental big cast iron three-D nutter.

NESBITT. Aye. And don't you ever forget it, *right*! (*Dougie jumps back.*) (*Winks to audience.*) Like that, eh? Wee bit of bravado there, know? (*Swigs, burps.*)

SCENE 5. Street.

Nesbitt lying, blootered, outside his house. Cans, an empty bottle of Buckfast, around him.

NESBITT. Coz I'll tell yi this, boy. See me . . . (*deep breath*) . . . I am not an alkie, by the way. Coz alkies get pisht and lie aboot the gutters. (*Takes a look around.*) I mean, fair enough, fair enough, I'm pisht and lying aboot the gutters, but I only do it casual. To them it's a day job, know? (*Takes a swig.*) Coz I only drink to be sociable, know? To pass myself in company. Coz I can take it or leave it . . . (*Another swig.*) I'd sooner take it all the same . . . (*He passes out*).

Gash and Burney appear, standing over him.

BURNEY. Christ, look at that, eh? Tell yi one thing. We musta been at the back of the queue the day role models were gied oot, eh?

GASH. Aye. One good thing though. At least he'll not take much living up to. You grab his arms, I'll get his legs.

BURNEY. Right.

Gash is stooped, about to take the legs. He sniffs something.

GASH. Tell yi what. Skip that. We'll just get an arm each.

They lift him towards the house. Mary appears at the front door. She wears a frilly nightie under her open coat. Man's socks, slippers, fag in mouth.

NESBITT. I'm awright, I'm awright . . .

MARY. And where'd yeez think yeez are going with that?

GASH. In the house. We're taking him up to his pit.

BURNEY. What've you got your nightgown on for, Maw? Yi got the flu?

MARY. No, I havnie got the flu! I was trying to put the bliddy sparkle back into my marriage!

NESBITT. Yi can easy do that, darling. Just nip up Oddbins and get iz a flagon of Strongbow.

MARY. Empty that oot upstairs afore it chokes on its own vomit.

GASH. Or mine. Have you put your snout near the crotch of his trousers lately?

BURNEY. If she'd done that, she widnae need to put the sparkle back into her marriage.

MARY. (*Scudding him.*) See you, wee yin, you know too bliddy much!

BURNEY. Aya!

GASH. You're not half sexy when you're angry, Maw.

MARY. (*Kicking ass.*) Do as yir bliddy well telt!

NESBITT. Youse heard yir mammy . . .

MARY. (*To Nesbitt, kicking.*) You tae!

NESBITT. Aya!

Mary turns to see a small knot of neighbours watching.

MARY. (*Shouting.*) Bugger aff . . . !

They scatter. She slams the door shut.

SCENE 6. The Nesbitts' living room.
Mary huddled over the fire, smoking, drinking tea, rocking slightly, back and forth. Gash and Burney with her. Gash sits at her feet, reading a book. Mary's hand occasionally playing through his hair. Burney sprawls on the settee opposite, regarding them. Mary is tense, fraught.

MARY. (*To Gash.*) There, y'see, son, let that be a lesson to yi. Never drink. You don't drink, do you, son?

GASH. No, Mammy, I don't drink.

BURNEY. Lying bastard.

GASH. (*To Burney.*) Shut it you, right! (*To Mary.*) No, Mammy, I don't even know the taste of the stuff.

MARY. That's good, son. Coz always remember. Just one drink

can put yi on the heartbreak road to misery and despair. (*Pause.*) Mind, it's awright in moderation . . .

A thump on the ceiling as if someone is falling out of bed.

(*Glancing skywards.*) Trouble is, your Da disnae know the meaning of the word.

BURNEY. Da disnae know the meaning of a lot of words. He cannie help it if he's a cretin.

GASH. Aye, trust you to stick up for him! Wee sook . . .

BURNEY. Sook? Look what's talking. Lying there on the carpet getting your belly tickled. Kidding on he's the man of the hoose.

GASH. I um the man of the hoose! When Da's blootered and oot the gemme, I um the man of the hoose, *right*?

BURNEY. Aye. The Dober-man maybes.

MARY. That's enough you two.

GASH. (*Points, threateningly.*) You're just jealous! Just watch it right!

He settles back, Mary strokes his hair again.

BURNEY. (*Watching.*) Some man. Look at it. Any minute noo she's gonny slip yi a worming pill and a box of Winnalot.

GASH. (*Exploding, throwing the book at him.*) I says bliddy watch it!

MARY. (*Scudding Gash.*) And I says pack it in! (*Scudding Burney.*) Pack it in, y'hear, both of yeez (*Breaking down.*) Can yeez not see I've got enough on my plate with that big eejit, without youse two knocking lumps oot of one another!

GASH. (*Touching her arm, hesitantly.*) There, there, Maw. It's awright . . . (*To Burney.*) Yi see what you've started noo?

BURNEY. Away and lick yourself . . . (*Still sprawled, unconcerned.*) There, there, Maw . . . (*Takes a draw at a fag.*)

NESBITT. (*Calls, from offstage.*) Mary! Mary!

MARY. Look, yeez are both big boys noo. And before yir Da comes doon I've something terrible to tell yeez. But yeez have to promise not to let on to him yeez know. (*Pause.*) Do yeez promise?

Gash and Burney look at each other.

GASH AND BURNEY. (*Together.*) Aye.

MARY. Well it's like this. Today, your Da found oot that unless he gies up the drink, he's only got . . . a year left to live.

Pause.

BURNEY. I see. And what's the something terrible?

GASH. (*With Mary.*) Shuttit you! Stop trying to act the hard man!

NESBITT. (*Shouting from offstage.*) Mary!!

GASH. (*To Mary.*) Never mind, Maw. Da's had a chance to sleep it off and let the news sink in. Maybe he'll come to his senses.

Door slams, offstage.

MARY. We'll soon find oot. Here he comes noo. Now remember your promise!

BURNEY. You can rely on me, Maw . . .

Door opens, Nesbitt enters, looking about.

NESBITT. Hullorerr, darling. I've a helluva thirst. Can yi lend iz a few bob for a swally?

GASH. (*To Mary.*) It was always a long shot . . .

BURNEY. (*Waves.*) Congratulations, Da! Happy birthday one-year-old!

Mary scuds him one.

Aya!

NESBITT. Cheers, son. Nae bother to yir old Da, eh? (*Rummaging about.*) Where's the purse then, Mary doll? Where've yi planked the dosh?

MARY. What dosh? It's all on my back! Look! (*Grabs nightie.*) A week's Family Allowance shot trying to put the bliddy glint of desire back into thae bloodshot eyeballs of yours!

BURNEY. Aye. We'll be on Spaghetti Hoops for a week so's you can get your oats.

MARY. (*Scudding him.*) Shuttit you!

BURNEY. Aya!

MARY. (*To Nesbitt.*) Though if I'd used my common sense I'd have saved my bliddy money to buy a shroud!

NESBITT. As long as it's white, Mary hen. Dark colours put half a stone on you. (*Moving Gash from chair.*) Shift your arse, Gash son . . .

MARY. It's not for me ya eejit, it's for you!

NESBITT. (*Feeling down the sides of the chair.*) Don't you worry about me, Mary hen. I'm awright, I'm awright . . . (*Finds a crumpled pound note, holds it aloft.*) Hull-o!

MARY. It's not you I'm worried aboot. It's these boys here. Whit's it gonny be like for them growing up withoot a faither!

BURNEY. Whit's the sweat? We've managed fine up till now.

GASH. (*Scudding him.*) Shuttit you.

BURNEY. (*Scudding him back.*) Don't *you* start!

NESBITT. Listen, doll, I'm not gonny trade slag offs with you at this juncture, know? Coz I'm a sunshine kinna guy. I need happy people aroon me. Now where's that effin purse afore I wreck the joint?

MARY. (*Picking up a poker.*) Bliddy well try it, Rab Nesbitt. You'll hit that furnance a dam't sight quicker than yi bargained for!

A ring at the doorbell. It's musical. It plays something with a drinking motif.

NESBITT. Ach suit yourself. I'm away oot to get blootered!

He storms out. Storms back in again.

But I'll tell yi this, lady. Yi can stick a sock in this body language carry on! Look at yi, swanking aboot there like a herry on hormones! Christ, if it was sex I was after I'd have picked Felicity Kendall or something. But no, no! Instead I done the decent thing and got latched onto something as pug ugly as myself! Christ, what's the point in getting married if yi canny take each other for granted? Ach, but that's the trouble with life these days. (*Storming out.*) Love's just a durty word . . .

Mary wipes away a tear.

BURNEY. There y'are, Maw. Who says romance is deid?

GASH. As a matter of interest, Maw. Where did yi plank the purse?

MARY. Take a tip, son. (*Feels uncomfortably about her person, produces purse.*) Never use cami-knickers as a deposit box.

Pulls relieved face.

SCENE 7. Lobby of house. Same moment.
Nesbitt heading for the door, shouting over his shoulder.

NESBITT. Coz if I want to bevvy, I'll bliddy well bevvy by the way! And you're not gonny sweet talk me off it, and no doctor's gonny bliddy well frighten me off it neither!

He opens the door quickly. Jamesie stands. Andra and Dodie are behind him at the foot of the path. Jamesie clutches a feather.

JAMESIE. Hi there, Rab. Fancy joining wur club?

NESBITT. Wit club?

JAMESIE. It's called the White Feather Club. It's for keech like wurselves that's shit scared of the drink, know?

They each hold two feathers before them in the shape of a cross and make a hissing noise.

We go for rambles and we get high on nature. And if any members brings a carry out he gets his heid stoved in with a Tizer bottle. Go on, Rab, what'd yi say?

NESBITT. (*Exploding.*) Bugger aff, that's what I say . . . !

He slams the door shut, Jamesie peeks through the letter box.

JAMESIE. Yi sure I canny tempt yi, Rab?

Nesbitt takes out a pencil.

NESBITT. C'mere, c'mere, c'mere . . . ! (*He hooks Jamesie's nose through the letter box with the pencil.*) No, yi canny bliddy well tempt me!

A pastoral scene – one man and his psychosis.

JAMESIE. Aya! Aya!

NESBITT. So just you take your bunch of chicken-feathered chicken hearts and get out of my bliddy face! Coz I am a Nesbitt, by the way! And a Nesbitt knows no fear! (*Slams box shut. To audience, panting.*) All this just coz I like a wee drink. Tell yi wan thing. All this shouting doesnie half give yi a drouth . . . (*Smacks his lips.*)

A strange hand proffers him a bottle. A voice speaks.

VOICE OF PINK ELEPHANT. That's the gemme, pal. You tell them. There's nothing the matter with a wee drink.

Nesbitt looks. A pink elephant stands.

NESBITT. (*Takes a drink.*) Who the hell are you by the way?

PINK ELEPHANT. Och come on, Rab. Use your imagination. I'm the heebie jeebies!

Nesbitt sprays out the drink.

Drink

SCENE 8. Doctor's surgery.
Doctor seated at desk, Nesbitt opposite, twisting his hands, anguished.

DOCTOR. An elephant, you say?

NESBITT. An elephant! A bliddy big pink elephant! As sure as you're sitting there. (*Reaching a hand across desk.*) That *is* you sitting there, by the way, in't it, Doctor?

DOCTOR. Of course.

NESBITT. Only after a whap to the brain like that, you tend not to take anything for granted any more, know what I mean?

DOCTOR. It's all in the mind, Mr Nesbitt.

NESBITT. Aye, I know. That's what worries me. It's a queer thing the mind, in't it? You never know what sleekit wee tricks it's gonny think up next, do you, eh?

DOCTOR. Then you should look after your body, Mr Nesbitt. Because a healthy body makes a healthy mind.

NESBITT. Christ, you're a right smug-faced bastard for a doctor, in't yi? I thought your job was to reassure the punters. Dish out a dod of the old bedside manner now and again. I mean, where's the drugs, by the way? I've kept my side of the bargain, I've brung yi the disease! Never mind bikes, is it not about time you got your arse in gear and did a bit of curing here?

DOCTOR. I've told you before, Mr Nesbitt. Nature provides the best cure. Your problem is getting the toxins out of your system. Not putting more in.

NESBITT. I see, I see. It's like that then is it, it's like that!

DOCTOR. But of course if you feel it's all too much for you, I could arrange for you to attend therapy sessions where you'd receive counselling and meet with other alcoholics who . . .

NESBITT. (*Rising, slamming fist on desk.*) I am not a bliddy alcoholic! And you can keep your therapy, boy. See, people like you, you get right on my nipple ends, so yeez do. (*Picking one up, waving it.*) All jumping aboot in your mincy wee running sannies, with your treacly wee words, with your 'therapy sessions' and your 'counselling'. Well I'll tell yi this boy, yi can ram your counselling right up your mileometer! Coz I will walk alone boy! I will do this my way! I don't need help from nobody! Nobody!

Nesbitt looks up. He sees, behind the doctor, the pink elephant standing, waving at him.

ELEPHANT. That's the gemme, Rab. You tell him.

NESBITT. (*Shudders, to doctor.*) What time's it start, by the way?

DOCTOR. Tomorrow morning, ten a.m.

NESBITT. I'll be there. (*Aggressively, to elephant.*) Gawn, get tae!

Nesbitt storms out. The doctor looks over his shoulder, sees nothing. He frowns, puzzled.

SCENE 9. Hospital. Therapy unit.

Ring of people seated. Nesbitt amongst them. They all wear lapel badges. Male counsellor seated in ring, white-coated, with clipboard, making notes.

NESBITT. (*To audience, mutters, nervous.*) Nice here in't it? Friendly like. I don't bliddy well think. This is how it must feel to be a number on a clock face.

COUNSELLOR. So to begin. Now we all know why we're here. Because we're all here for the same reason. Because we have a drink problem. Does everyone accept that?

They all, including Nesbitt, look amongst themselves, muttering awkward agreement. Nesbitt clocks the prim woman from the bus queue. He does a double take.

NESBITT. (*Clocking her.*) Awright, doll? Nearly didnae recognise yi there with your eyes focused!

She looks away, mortified.

Suit yirself, suit yirself . . . (*To audience.*) Fair broke the ice there, didn't I, eh?

COUNSELLOR. Good. Well perhaps we should try and get to know one another. And we can begin by telling the group a little bit about ourselves. Now who'd like to start us off? Let's see . . .

The counsellor's finger hovers in the air. It's about to alight on Nesbitt. Nesbitt raps his fist into his open palm. The counsellor's finger alights elsewhere, hurriedly.

Drink

COUNSELLOR. Graham. How about you?

The counsellor's gaze has settled on a dull-looking middle-aged man.

NESBITT. (*To audience.*) Hope he's not one of thae long-winded articles. My nerves are shrieking for a pint.

GRAHAM. (*Long, drawn out.*) Well . . . I suppose the cause of my drinking lies in my childhood. And in some ways even before that. You see, it all began with my great great grandfather . . .

NESBITT. (*To audience.*) One good thing aboot spending your entire life queuing up in the social security. Yi learn how to sleep with your eyes open . . .

He looks up at the clock. We see that it's 10.30. Nesbitt slumps back in his chair, a faraway look in his eyes.

We see the clock again.

It's 11.05.

Graham's voice drones on. Nesbitt is getting anxious. He twists his hands.

GRAHAM. So gradually I got over the genetic scarring on that portion of my racial memory. But then came my grandfather . . .

NESBITT. And was your grandfather as big a pain in the onions as you are?

GRAHAM. I'm sorry, but I'm on medication. I can't deal with hostility. Would somebody speak to him please?

PRIM WOMAN. Graham's right. He's done nothing but show aggression since he came in here. Why are you so negative?

NESBITT. Who says I'm negative just coz I show aggression?

THIRD GROUP MEMBER. He should be asked to leave. He's upsetting group harmony.

NESBITT. (*Showing a fist.*) I'll upset more than group harmony in a minute, boy!

A spot of alarm, generally.

COUNSELLOR. Calm down please everyone! (*To Nesbitt.*) Look Robert, why are you behaving this way? You want to be cured of your drinking problem, don't you?

Nesbitt doesn't answer.

Well, don't you?

NESBITT. (*Springing up.*) No, I bliddy well don't, by the way! Coz see me, by the way, I love drinking! Drink's my life! If it wisnae for the prospect of a good bucket, I'd have no reason to get up in the morning! And I'll tell yi this, I might only hae a stinking year left to live, but I'm gonny pour that twelve month into one big glass, (*produces an aerosol can from pocket*) and I'm gonny put it to my lips (*takes top off*) and I'm gonny drink it, there y'are! Coz the only harmony I'm interested in, is Harmony bliddy hair spray there y'are! And I'll tell yeez, I maybes not have the best liver in Glesga, but I bet I've got the silkiest and most manageable! Gawn . . . !

He goes.

GRAHAM. You know, in a ghastly way, I can't help admiring him.

PRIM WOMAN. I know. It's like the Charge of the Light Brigade, isn't it. Stupid, but magnificent . . .

They all look towards the door.

NESBITT. (*At door, calls back.*) Cheers!

He squirts some hairspray into his mouth. He burps, exits. The doors swing back and forth.

SCENE 10. Outside. Day.
Nesbitt's sitting somewhere, but we don't yet see where. He speaks to the audience.

NESBITT. That's me, by the way, love a wee bit of theatre, know? A wee Florentine gesture, once in a while. Coz see when yi get down to it, I don't half talk some amount of keech. Coz I'll admit it, I'm as feart of punting the pail as the next man. I mean, look at this. See this . . . ?

We look. He is in a park, on the grass, pouring Irn Bru into a paper cup. Mary's nearby, making jam sandwiches.

This is me, a week without a bevvy. Cross my heart. (*He tries to cross himself, spills the contents.*) Oh, Christ! See all this? Govan picnic, by the way. Bottle of Irn Bru, ten fags and two weans, know. (*Shouts.*) Hey youse! Hey youse! Gie that wumman back her zimmer!

Gash and Burney. They're teasing an old woman. They have her walking frame. She crawls along behind them, trying to get it back. Hearing Nesbitt shout, they chuck it down.

BURNEY. But Da, we're bored!

NESBITT. Never mind bored! There'll be plenty time for boredom when you're my age! (*To audience.*) That's the trouble with life. Once you realise you're never gonny be a somebody, yi have to kid yourself on that being a naebody can still be interesting. So is it any wonder us low forms of life gets blootered. No' that I drink, by the way. I'm off the drink. See me, I widnae thank yi for a drink. I . . . I . . . (*He halts in mid-phrase. He sniffs the air. He looks right, straining his eyes, to the far horizon.*)

We see a pub.

Nesbitt shudders at the sight.

NESBITT. (*To audience, wringing his hands.*) Bugger it. I want a drink!

He spots Mary's bag on the ground, does a double take

We clock the bag. We see Mary's purse sticking out.

MARY. (*Proffering sandwich.*) This is rerr, so it is, Rab. Having a picnic, just like a normal family. Are yi enjoying yourself?

NESBITT. (*Wringing his hands.*) Aye, I'm delirious, delirious . . .

MARY. Don't be so sarcastic!

NESBITT. I'm not being sarcastic, I'm delirious, believe me!

MARY. I don't understand your moods sometimes. I wisht you'd join in a bit!

Gash and Burney run up.

BURNEY. Hey, Da. This picnic's minging! Gonny gie us a game at something?

NESBITT. What? Go on, beat it and gie's peace! (*Has a rethink.*) No, tell you what, son. That's a good idea. We'll have a wee game of hide and seek, okay?

Enthusiasm from Gash and Burney.

D'yi fancy, Mary?

MARY. Might as well. If it lifts the curse off your fizzog.

NESBITT. Right, I'll hide first. All youse shut yir peepers and count to twenty, slow, awright!

ALL. (*Covering their eyes.*) Right. (*Counting.*) One, two, three . . .

Nesbitt stoops, picks up the purse.

NESBITT. (*To Gash and Burney.*) Nae peeking noo . . . (*To audience.*) Weans are that trusting, aren't they?

Nesbitt legs it in the direction of the pub.

GASH AND BURNEY. Eight, nine, ten . . .

They peek.

BURNEY. (*To Gash.*) Predictable big eejit, isn't he?

GASH. He's not the only one. Any second now . . .

MARY. (*Shouts.*) Hey, ya durty big midden! Come back here!

NESBITT. (*Shouts back.*) Aye, right, so I will! (*To audience.*) Stupid thing to shout that, in't it?

He turns to resume running, bumps into the old woman with the zimmer.

Struggling past her.

Gawn, get to! Creeping aboot all over the place! (*Runs on.*)

MARY. (*Shouts.*) Just you wait!

BURNEY. (*To Gash.*) That kinna takes the guesswork oot it, doesn't it?

SCENE 11. A street with trees. That evening.
Andra, Jamesie and Dodie standing by a tree.

DODIE. Tell yi something. Yi get fed up with this rambling carry on. All this green stuff looks the same.

ANDRA. What'd they call this big effort here?

JAMESIE. (*Regarding it.*) I think it's some kinna tree. But don't quote me . . . . Look, there's Rab.

Nesbitt passes, fish supper in hand.

Where yi been, Rab? We huvnie seen yi for a while.

NESBITT. (*Without stopping.*) A picnic.

JAMESIE. That's nice. And did yi enjoy it?

NESBITT. (*Walking on.*) Mind your own business, ya wee teatotal toe-rag yi.

JAMESIE. (*To others.*) I'm please I asked there. Fair put my mind at rest, know?

DODIE. (*To Jamesie and Andra.*) I'm sick of being at one with nature. Who needs inner peace? Why don't we just go hame and watch Telly Addicts?

ANDRA. Might as well. After all, what's nature ever done for us?

JAMESIE. Not a thing. (*Kicks tree.*) Dirty big green swine!

They all kick the tree. Venting their frustrations.

ANDRA. Boot him on the roots!

DODIE. Intae him! Chib his foliage! Get ya . . . !

SCENE 12. Street near Nesbitt's house. Same time.
Nesbitt staggering towards his house.

NESBITT. (*To audience.*) What you looking at? Don't talk to me . . . . Awright! Awright! Awright! So I'm in the wrong . . . But that's not my fault, is it? No, I'll tell yeez, it's your bliddy fualt, that's whose fault it is! Stands to reason, din't it? I mean. It's stress that makes me bevvy. And stress is caused by society. And all youse people is society. *So it's your bliddy fualt I knocked her purse!* Gawn, get to! You're nothing but a lot of tea leafs the lot of yeez! Preying on helpless scum. See, that's my trouble. (*He's at his door. He presses the doorbell.*) Know my trouble? I'm just the innocent victim of a guilty conscience, that's my trouble . . .

Light is switched on in the passageway. We see it through the glass.

(*To audience.*) Watch this. I'll need to play this a bit shrewd, know? A bit intelligent. Give it the old boyish charm with a wee dod of spiritual torment round the eyeballs, know? I mean, be honest. That's why yi make somebody love yi. So yi can exploit it . . .

Door opens. Mary stands. Nesbitt stoops, humble.

(*With hands outstretched.*) Mary, doll . . . I've been a bad man. What can I say?

MARY. What can you say? You can start with 'ouch'.

She hits him over the head with an Irn Bru bottle.

SCENE 13. Doctor's surgery.
Close up on Nesbitt as the doctor dabs at his scalp with iodine.

NESBITT. Aya! Aya! Keep the heid will yi, keep the heid!

DOCTOR. Honestly, the lives you people lead. You don't deserve a health service.

NESBITT. Just shut up and keep prodding, will yi. My heid's louping. I don't need your patter.

DOCTOR. Well you won't have to put up with it much longer if you continue the way you're going.

NESBITT. I tried to gie up the drink, man. But I had to go back on it again. Sobriety was playing havoc with my sex life!

DOCTOR. Really? How so?

NESBITT. It was her, man. She said the foreplay wasnie worth a tosser since my hands stopped shaking.

DOCTOR. A likely story. You'll blame anything but yourself, won't you.

He sits at his desk.

NESBITT. Whit'd yi mean, whit'd yi mean?

DOCTOR. Take a long hard look at yourself, Nesbitt. You're gross. You're unfit. You wouldn't know a diet sheet from a bed sheet. You've abused your body systematically since adulthood. You're the living embodiment of a working class sloth, ignorance and hedonistic self-indulgence that borders on the obscene.

NESBITT. I see, I see. We'll don't hold back, will you . . .

DOCTOR. Just look at the difference between us, man! We're

about the same age, but I've looked after myself! I don't smoke, drink, I've a daily regime of exercise. And as a result I've the same waist size I had when I was twenty-one.

NESBITT. Well so have I! (*Tugging at waistband.*) I was always a fat bastard!

DOCTOR. I don't know why I bother. You people are incorrigible. (*Uncomprehending look from Nesbitt.*) It means you're too stupid to change. (*Rising.*) Now if you'd excuse me, I'd like to get a couple of . . .

The doctor gasps, chokes, having a heart attack. He falls, kneeling, grasping at Nesbitt's feet. Nesbitt stands, regarding him.

NESBITT. Aye, you see? Yi would open yir big mooth, wouldn't yi?

The doctor gurgles, eyes popping. Nesbitt lifts the doctor's hand, places it against his string vest.

There y'are, feel that, pal! Strong as an ox and with an IQ to match! There's no justice, is there?

The doctor slumps back, dead.

NESBITT. (*Looking skyward.*) Allow you, big yin. You've got a sense of humour after all! This calls for a drink! (*Raises iodine bottle.*) Cheers!

He's about to drink when the pink elephant looms up at his shoulder.

ELEPHANT. That's it, Rab. You get it down yi. It'll do yi good.

NESBITT. (*Shudders.*) Maybes I'll just have a cuppa tea when I get hame!

A receptionist enters, screams.

NESBITT. (*Exciting.*) It's awright, doll. It's not all bad news. Tell his wife I'll buy his trainers off him. (*Calls.*) Get that kettle on, Mary, I'm jogging hame!

SCENE 14. Street. Day.
Nesbitt comes puffing into view, up a hill. He wears running gear. He's timing himself.

NESBITT. (*Aloud.*) One minute fifty-two, one minute fifty-three, one minute fif . . .

James Aaron Cotter – This is Your Life.

Jamesie, close by, sitting on a bench, drinking from a bottle. He clocks Nesbitt.

JAMESIE. (*Shouts.*) Hey, Rab! Whit yi creeping about in yir underwear for? Yi sleep-walking or something?

NESBITT. (*Stops, points.*) Just watch it, Cotter. Coz I'll tell yi this! I'll tell yi this! I'll . . . On second thoughts I'll tell yi nothing. (*To audience.*) Got to watch my blood pressure, know?

He puts on Walkman headphones, runs on.

The Pink Elephant appears.

ELEPHANT. (*To audience.*) That's the great thing aboot life. When one mooth closes, another opens . . .

The elephant slides along the bench up to Jamesie, puts an arm round him.

(*To Jamesie.*) Hullorerr, pal. D'yi come here often?

JAMESIE. (*Not looking.*) Aye, now and again. Whit about yir . . .

He looks, does a double take. A look of alarm spreads across his face, slowly.

114

Rab C. Nesbitt

EPISODE FIVE

CAST LIST

SHUG	Sean Scanlan
PHOEBE	Sara Corper
MARY NESBITT	Elaine C. Smith
FIRST POLICEMAN	Bill Barclay
JAMESIE COTTER	Tony Roper
RAB C. NESBITT	Gregor Fisher
BURNEY	Eric Cullen
GASH	Andrew Fairlie
FOURTH POLICEMAN	Andy Gray
PASSER-BY	Russell Horton
ANGIE'S MOTHER	Anne Kristen
ANDRA	Iain McColl
DODIE	Brian Pettifer
DESK SERGEANT	Stephen Greif
GIRL WITH BABY	Melissa Wilks

Rab C. Nesbitt

SCENE 1. Prissy-looking house in Sidcup. Day.
*Long shot of prissy-looking house in Sidcup. (A bungalow or a semi.)
There's a newish-looking car in the driveway, garden furniture on the
lawn. We hear a telephone bleeping, loudly, instantly, from within.
We see Shug, a man in his fifties, in cardigan, standing at the
window, a bag of golf clubs by him.*

*Inside we see the telephone on its chintzy little table, ringing its head
off. Phoebe, Shug's wife, goes to answer it, peeling off rubber gloves.
Shug wheels round from the window. He's fondling a putter,
compulsively.*

SHUG. Stop!

PHOEBE. (*Startled.*) What?

SHUG. Don't answer that phone.

PHOEBE. But Hugh, it's ringing!

SHUG. I know it's ringing. I know that ring. It's a special ring. A
ring known only to me. Don't answer that ring, Phoebe.

PHOEBE. (*With hand resting on receiver.*) Hugh . . . Is there
something you haven't told me about yourself?

SHUG. I'm afraid so, Phoebe. For a start, my name isn't Hugh.

PHOEBE. Not Hugh? Then who . . .

SHUG. You . . . don't need to know that. But since we've been
married for thirteen years, I suppose you're due some sort of
explanation.

PHOEBE. Go on . . .

SHUG. Well, you remember I told you I was a lonely orphan
from Berwick-on-Tweed, whose only relative was tragically killed
when some vandals put skateboards under a heffer?

PHOEBE. Yes.

SHUG. Well, it was lies. My family weren't bide-a-wees from the
Cheviot Valley. We were by-the-ways from Giro Valley. I'm
talking the Govan dust bowl. Phoebe, I'm scum.

PHOEBE. Shush, the neighbours . . . But why didn't you tell me
before?

SHUG. How could I? You thought I was a somebody. That I was used to money. But when I first came down here I had nothing but my own wits, a masonic handshake, and an ingratiating manner to back me up. On top of that, I was ashamed of my own family!

PHOEBE. That's a terrible thing to say.

SHUG. You think so? (*Shows.*) Here's their picture.

PHOEBE. God! Maybe they'll look better once they've evolved.

SHUG. They're ghastly Phoebe, but they're all I've got. That's why whenever I hear that phone ring in a secret way, I know one of them needs me and I'm duty bound to help.

PHOEBE. I see. But tell me. If your name isn't Hugh . . .

SHUG. It *is* Hugh.

PHOEBE. But I don't understand. You said . . .

SHUG. I don't understand either, Phoebe, God knows! But for some idiotic reason when you're given the name Hugh up there, you don't get called Hugh. Instead they call you . . .

SCENE 2. The Nesbitts' living room. Same moment.
The Nesbitt living room. Mary Nesbitt, phone in hand. A rammy audible from without. Nesbitt dashing about behind her, stuffing clothes into a suitcase.

MARY. (*Shouting into phone.*) Shug! Shug! For Christ's sake will yi pick up your phone!

SCENE 3. Outside the Nesbitts' front door. Same moment.
The Nesbitts' front door. Police car parked on pavement. Three policemen battering at door. Policeman 1, a sergeant. A fourth struggling with a ladder.

FIRST POLICEMAN. Let us in Nesbitt. I've got a warrant here! Sixteen charges of non-payment of fines. You're bliddy huckled! Open up!

Letter box opens. Jamesie shouts through.

JAMESIE. Beat it! We don't want any Tupperware!

FIRST POLICEMAN. (*To others.*) Right boys, that is it. Apply the footwear!

They boot the door.

Inside in the lobby. Jamesie, Dodie and Andra, holding the door. Shouting from the police outside.

JAMESIE. (*To Andra and Dodie.*) Hold on boys, hold on! (*Shouts through.*) For God's sake, Mary hen, get a move on! Have yi not got his case packed yet?

Mary still holding the phone. Nesbitt scuttling about, stuffing clothes into the suitcase. We hear the phone ringing tone down the line.

NESBITT. (*Shouting back.*) I'm having to do it my bliddy self, by the way! That's too busy gassing to its bliddy relations on the phone!

MARY. I'm not gassing! I'm trying to get through to our Shug to get you a safe hoose to hole up in! (*Fraught.*) C'mon, Shug . . . C'mon . . . !

NESBITT. Safe hoose! Probably a bliddy Wendy hoose knowing that anglified stuck-up swine.

MARY. Shug's got on in life! Not like me. And get that bliddy bandage changed. You're not giving me a showing-up down there!

NESBITT. (*Skiting her hand away.*) Get your paws aff! I change this headgear for nobody! London can take me as it finds me!

JAMESIE. (*Shouts through.*) That's if the busys don't find yi first! Will yi get a bliddy move on!

NESBITT. Aye, I'm gawn, I'm gawn . . . ! (*Mutters.*) Where's my bliddy strap. Ach . . . ! (*He whips off his belt as if to lash it around the case.*)

Outside, same moment. Upstairs window of Nesbitt's house. We see Gash at the window. He's clutching a letter. We see him scream, inaudibly, through the glass.

SCENE 4. Inside the Nesbitts' house. Upstairs bedroom. Day.
Gash at window screaming. He gives three long screams before Burney, who's sitting in bed, reading a DSS leaflet, smoking, acknowledges Gash's noise.

BURNEY. (*Casually.*) Something the matter?

GASH. (*Sits on bed.*) No, nothing's the matter. And if there was I wouldn't tell you anyway!

BURNEY. You wouldn't need to. I can guess. It's that letter, isn't it?

GASH. (*Clutching the letter to his chest.*) The bitch! She didnae even have the guts to tell me to my face!

BURNEY. Can yi blame her? Who'd want to watch a wimp squealing? Anyway, I don't know what you're getting all upset about. It was only a holiday romance.

GASH. It wisnae a holiday romance! It was a work romance. Three months on a youth scheme scrubbing out pensioners' patios! (*Catch in voice.*) We were bonded by suds. (*Producing squeazy.*) Even now, I sleep with her squeazy sponge under my pillow. It's a funny thing, but sometimes I'll pass a shop doorway and get the whang of Flash from a mop bucket and instinctively I'll stop and waggle my toes, expecting to find them squidgy again, through the holes in my trainers. Silly, isn't it?

BURNEY. 'Squidgy'. Is that one of her 'London' words?

GASH. Angie taught me the meaning of a lot of words. Excitement. Freedom . . .

BURNEY. Dumped.

GASH. I was not dumped! She had to go back hame, she got a place at Uni! It was just like her to go bumming around Europe on her jack. She even thought of going to the Third World, and working with lepers.

BURNEY. Instead she came to Govan and worked with pensioners. Same difference. What yi blubbing for?

GASH. (*Wiping tear.*) I'm not blubbing. I've just got a sty coming in my eye. (*Choked.*) I canny believe I'll not see her again!

BURNEY. Well don't give up hope. Try reading between the lines. What's the letter say?

GASH. (*Reads a little.*) There is no hope. Don't try reading between the lines. It's best we should part this way. Regards, Angie. What'd yi think?

Rab C. Nesbitt

BURNEY. Well it wasnie just the one regard. At least she sent a few of them.

GASH. (*Leaping up.*) I've got to speak to her again! I'll go mental if I don't!

BURNEY. Forget it. You're wasting your time.

GASH. You don't understand! At least there was hope when she was around. Nothing ever happens in this doss hole!

A pane of the window is smashed. The fourth policeman looks in. He's on a ladder.

FOURTH POLICEMAN. Hey, youse! Where's your bliddy faither?

BURNEY. Out, making an arse of you lot. Where's yours?

FOURTH POLICEMAN. Less of your lip! Here, when yi see him give him this. (*Chucks it in.*) It's a warrant for his arrest!

BURNEY. (*Catches it.*) Cheers. I'll put it with the others. (*Opens*

I like this shot. Kinna natural looking, know?

drawer to reveal pile.) I hope you're gonny fix that windae, by the way!

FOURTH POLICEMAN. (*Regarding the cardboard patches.*) I'll send yi another egg box in the morning . . .

BURNEY. Aye, yi better, or I'll be seeing my child psychologist aboot you! (*Turns to Gash.*) Showed that tube, din't I, eh . . . haw? Haw . . . ?

No Gash. He looks to the door in time to see Gash's back disappearing, suitcase in hand.

Door slams shut.

SCENE 5. Back door of the Nesbitts' house. Day.
Policeman's ladder visible. Door flies open. Nesbitt hurries out, holding up trousers with one hand, suitcase in the other.

NESBITT. (*Shouts back into house.*) Cheerio, doll! I'll gie yi a ring when I get to London!

Fourth Policeman up the ladder.

FOURTH POLICEMAN. (*Shouts.*) Boys! He's round the back and he's going to London!

NESBITT. (*Shouts back into house.*) I mean Aberdeen, doll! Aberdeen!

FOURTH POLICEMAN. (*Shouts.*) Boys, he's going to London and he's kidding on it's Aberdeen!

NESBITT. (*To Fourth Policeman.*) Why don't you shut your stupid yap!

He gives the ladder a quick wrench. It falls. Fourth Policeman hangs dangling from the window ledge.

(*To audience.*) I'm getting too old for all this malarkey . . .

He throws his case over the wall, climbs after it.

SCENE 6. The Nesbitts' living room. Day.
Same moment. Mary on the phone. Burney lounging on settee, smoking.

MARY. (*Into phone.*) Thanks, Shug. He's just going down on a business trip. You'll hardly know he's there.

She puts the phone down. Door bursts open as she does so. The police loom in. She picks up a poker, wields it.

(*To police shouting.*) Aye, that's right! Come bursting in here, harassing decent people! Polis? (*Spits.*) You're a waste of bliddy space, the lot of yeez!

BURNEY. (*Casually.*) Oh that reminds me, Maw. Oor Gash's ran away to England, by the way, and he's never coming back.

MARY. He's what? Oh my God . . .

BURNEY. I forgot to mention and that. Sorry.

MARY. (*To policeman, wielding poker.*) Well don't just stand there! Spin roon on yir ribtappers and let's see a crush of serge at that door! Fun my bliddy wean . . . !

A crush of serge at the door.

BURNEY. (*To audience.*) Homely bitch, isn't she? (*Scud across the head.*) Aya!

SCENE 7. Victoria Coach Station. Day.
Nesbitt emerging from the station, suitcase in hand.

NESBITT. (*To audience.*) Look at this, eh? The London! Some place London, boy, eh? Finest sight a Scotsman ever sees! Tell yi wan thing. See the bam that said that? Probably living in some castle up in Dumfries noo. Hypocritical bastard. All the same, really oozes class, doesn't it, eh?

A crippled beggar lies propped and filthy against a wall.

(*To beggar.*) Awright there, pal? (*Points.*) No legs, eh? (*Giving thumbs up.*) Good career move! (*To audience, moving on.*) See what I mean? Pure gold! Yi canny buy that . . .

He accosts a middle class-looking passer by. A black man is sweeping the streets close by.

NESBITT. (*To passer by.*) Excuse me, Jim. (*Shows crumpled piece of paper.*) I'm trying to get oot to Sidcup, know? The wife's cousin's gonny gie iz a billet like. What's the way oot there and that, know?

SUBTITLE. Pardon me, can you direct me to Sidcup?

PASSER BY. What?

Offski

Posing shamelessly for the tourists. Well, they're mostly yanks and they get confused if we don't conform to stereotype.

NESBITT. Sidcup and that! I'm trying to get oot to Sidcup!

PASSER BY. (*Going to move off.*) I'm sorry, I can't understand what you're saying . . .

NESBITT. Oh, is that a fact? Hey, c'mere. C'mere! Canny understand what I'm saying, eh? Well let me ask yi, have yi seen the telly? Have yi seen *Neighbours*?

PASSER BY. *Neighbours*? Yes.

NESBITT. And did yi understand that?

PASSER BY. Of course.

NESBITT. Well that's queer, by the way. Coz they're bliddy Australians, halfway doon the other end of the planet! Christ, I'm just up the road in Glesga! So if yi can understand them, boy, yi can understand me! So in future clean yir bliddy ears oot! Gawn, on yir way! Ignorant bamstick . . .

Passer by moves off, fast. Nesbitt spots the black guy, who's been watching.

(*To black guy.*) And I don't know what you're bliddy grinning at! It's awright for youse. At least they gie youse menial jobs to do. Christ, up there we've got bugger all! I'll tell yi, black is it? Black? Christ I'm blacker than you are pal, and I'm white, there y'are! (*Turns away, turns back.*) Afore I go, gie's five by the way.

They slap skin.

(*To audience.*) I always wanted to do that, know!

SCENE 8. Shug's living room. Day.
Shug at the window, peering out intently. Phoebe, sitting, inserting a Radio Times into its leather binder, sees him, gets annoyed.

PHOEBE. Hugh, if you must stand at the window, try and look angst ridden. At least let the neighbours think our relationship has a dynamic.

SHUG. I am angst ridden. My stomach's in knots through tension. God knows what's going to come staggering down that street.

PHOEBE. (*Going to him.*) Oh, don't be so intolerant. After all Glasgow's the City of Culture now. Some of it's bound to have rubbed off on the . . . tribespeople.

SHUG. Yes, I suppose so. It's just that I've worked so hard to squeeze the Scottishness out of my system. In fact, only last week the Club greenkeeper paid me the ultimate compliment.

PHOEBE. What was that?

SHUG. He said he thought I was a Medway man.

PHOEBE. (*Taking his hand.*) And one day, Hugh, you will be . . . !

A knock at the window. They look, startled. A face looms, grinning. It's Nesbitt.

NESBITT. (*Through the window.*) Awright there, doll? Rab C. Nesbitt, fae Govan! (*Holding up a bottle of Buckfast, some Export cans.*) Hey Shug, 'Mon get blootered!

SCENE 9. Shug's living room. Day.
Nesbitt occupying an armchair. Shug and Phoebe sit on the settee, rather tentatively, watching him.

NESBITT. (*Belches.*) Don't drink? Whit'd yi mean yi don't drink?

He kicks off his trainers beside a tall potted plant.

SHUG. I mean I used to drink, Rab. In the old days I'd 'go my bucket' with the best of them. But I've given it up.

PHOEBE. (*Gripping Shug's hand.*) He's seen the misery it brings.

NESBITT. Aye, I can see he looks a lot happier teetotal, by the way.

He swigs from a can. A cuckoo clock strikes above his head, startling him.

(*Spraying out beer.*) What the f . . . !

Shug and Phoebe laugh lightly.

PHOEBE. Don't be alarmed, Rob. It's just a little *object d'art* we picked up on a sojourn to the Black Forest.

SHUG. You'll get used to it!

NESBITT. (*Eyeing it.*) Want to bliddy well bet? (*To clock.*) Get to . . . !

Telephone rings, Phoebe rises to answer. Shug leans across quickly, speaks so that Phoebe can't hear. His anglified accent slips, somewhat.

SHUG. Listen, Rab. I don't mean to be nosy, but you're not doon here coz you're in any kinna bother with the polis, are yi?

NESBITT. What? No, no! In fact I can honestly say that I've took steps to *avoid* having trouble with the polis, know? (*Sips.*) No, I'm just doing a wee bit of sightseeing, know?

SHUG. Sightseeing? I thought Mary said it was a business trip?

NESBITT. Oh it is, it is! See I'm in the sightseeing business, yi see?

Phoebe on the phone.

PHOEBE. (*Into receiver.*) Mary? Oh, *that* Mary! What's wrong?

SCENE 10. The Nesbitts' living room. Day.
Mary on phone, tearful, fag and Carlsberg Special in free hand. Burney hovers in the background looking slightly miffed.

MARY. Oh, Phoebe, Phoebe, it's my wean! I'm pure like that, so I am! He's shot the craw, I'm up to high doh! Christ knows whit the score is!

SUBTITLE. My child has run away, I am very worried.

SCENE 11. Shug's living room. Same moment. Day.

NESBITT. (*To Shug.*) Aye, see I'm a kinna on site sightseer, know? I see the site, then I see the sights on the site, then if there's any good sights I see the overseer aboot the sights I've seen on the site, know?

SHUG. (*Doubtfully.*) I see.

NESBITT. And I'll tell yi something else an' all.

SHUG. What's that?

NESBITT. I huvne half seen some sights!

PHOEBE. (*To Nesbitt, phone in hand.*) Rob! Rob; it's for you. It's Mary. I think there's something wrong.

NESBITT. (*Rising.*) Mary? What is it, what's up?

PHOEBE. I don't know, I can't understand what she's saying.

NESBITT. What?

PHOEBE. (*Louder.*) I said I can't understand what she's saying.

NESBITT. (*To Phoebe, taking phone.*) It's no use doll, I canny understand what you're saying . . . (*Mutters to audience.*) They'll get bliddy sick of it afore I do . . . (*Into phone.*) Mary, what's the score hen? (*Slight pause.*) Ran away? Where's he ran away to? London? Och well that's no bother. That's just doon the road from Sidcup . . .

Shug and Phoebe exchange a look.

I'll just nick into London later on and get him. And I'll tell yi, see when I see him, he's for a right good kicking, by the way! A right good pummelling! Och aye, I'll give him a big hug first. I mean I'm his father! Right Mary hen, awrabest, cheerio!

He hangs up. Turns to Shug and Phoebe.

Women, eh? She's in some state thee. All because wee Gash has ran away!

PHOEBE. I'm not surprised, Rob. London's one of the biggest cities in the world. He could be anywhere!

Offski

SHUG. Phoebe's right, Rab. There's more people in Greater London than there are in the whole of Scotland!

NESBITT. Oh aye. But it's quality that coonts, not quantity . . . Whit'd yi think I should do well?

SHUG. There's only one thing to do . . .

PHOEBE. You'll have to go to the police.

NESBITT. (*Swaying, gripping the furniture.*) Christ . . .

SHUG. What's the matter, Rab. Are you feeling unwell?

NESBITT. Nah, nah, I'm awright. Just a wee tate of jet lag, know. If yeeze don't mind, I think I'll just mosey away up to my scratcher. G'night . . .

SHUG AND PHOEBE. (*Together.*) G'night, Rab . . . Rob.

He goes.

PHOEBE. (*To Shug.*) What'd you reckon, Hugh? D'you think they'll find that boy?

SHUG. I'd say there's a fair chance. If he's anything like his father, all they need to do is follow their noses . . .

He stoops to pick up Nesbitt's trainers. We see that the plant has keeled over, dead. Shug holds out the trainers, sniffs them from a distance, pulls a face . . .

SCENE 12. Street billboard. Day.
Large billboard. It shows Conservative Party Conference poster 1989.

Gash lying beneath it, curled up, asleep. A Gleaves tyupe figure in a Salvation Army-looking uniform stops by Gash. Stands, looking down at him. He unfolds a blanket, places it gently over Gash. Gash opens his eyes, slowly.

GASH. (*Exhausted.*) Sally Army? Thanks, mister. That's the first kindness anybody's showed me since I arrived in this city.

The Gleaves type smiles benignly, looks about, sees the coast is clear, removes his hat, climbs quickly in beside Gash.

GASH. (*As realisation dawns.*) Get to! Mammy, Daddy!

He scarpers. The Gleaves type puts his hat back on, full of annoyance and disappointment. We see the headband reads 'Salacious Army'.

127

SCENE 13. Street/large house. Day.
It's raining. Gash stumbles up a well-to-do street. He's tired, wet, dispirited. He stops by a large house, consults the crumpled letter in his hand. Satisfied it's the right address, he regards the house, a little daunted.

GASH. (*Regarding.*) Christ!

He walks up the path. The curtain flickers. A hatchet-faced looking middle class woman peeks out.

Gash rings the doorbell.

GASH. Non musical? Now that's what I call class . . .

The door opens. The hatchet-faced woman appears.

HATCHET FACE. Yes?

GASH. Eh, hullo, missus. I was just passing. My name's Gash Nesbitt. I'm a friend of Angie's. (*Proffers hand.*)

HATCHET FACE. (*Ignoring hand.*) Angela? *My* Angela knows *you*?

GASH. Aye. We worked together in Glesga like, know?

HATCHET FACE. (*Mystery explained.*) Ah . . . Well Angela isn't here during term time. She's at the Halls of Residence at University.

GASH. I see. What university is she at? Maybes I could be 'just passing' that as well, know?

HATCHET FACE. I doubt it. Unless you can walk on water. She's at the University of Salzburg.

Puzzled frown from Gash.

In Austria.

GASH. Oh, I see. (*Lets it sink in.*) Well, missus, I'll tell yi this. I'm keen. But I'll be Donald Ducked if I'm gonny yodel for any bint!

HATCHET FACE. What?

GASH. Nothing. (*Goes to turn away, turns back.*) Listen missus, see me? I'm cold, I'm tired, I'm wet and I'm hungry. As one human being to another . . .

HATCHET FACE. (*Coldly.*) Yes?

GASH. Skip it . . . Just crack your face and make your arse jealous, wid yi . . .

Door slams shut.

(*Winks to audience.*) Magic gesture, eh? (*Shivers, pulls up collar.*) Hope it's worth hypothermia . . . (*Shuffles off.*)

SCENE 14. Front step of Jamesie's house. Day.
Close-up on a lurid headline in the Star. *Pull out to show front step of Jamesie's house. Jamesie, Andra and Dodie sitting together on the step, pouring wine into cups.*

JAMESIE. (*Proffering.*) There y'are boys, get that down yi . . .

ANDRA. Cheers, Jamesie. Hey nae offence and that. But I hope this isnae South African?

JAMESIE. Certainly not, Andra! I mean it's up to us developed nations to set an example. Help the world's oppressed, know?

ANDRA. Exactly! (*Sips.*) Christ, in't this not a typical Glesga day, eh? Look at it. Sky the colour of mouldy breid. Deid cat hinging from a lampost. Disposable nappies splattering on the gutter from the one-parent hostel next door . . .

We hear one do so.

DODIE. You're right. (*Trembling lip.*) My God, I love this country! You know, when yi get right doon to it, we've maybes no' got much. But at least we've got one another, eh?

ANDRA. Friendship, big man. I'll drink to that!

JAMESIE. Hey, hey. (*Punching his heart.*) And let's not forget absent friends, know?

ANDRA AND DODIE. (*Toasting.*) Absent friends . . .

DODIE. Christ, you're fair taking it hard in't yi, Jamesie?

JAMESIE. Listen, when Rab went a part of me died. (*Glances.*) Look, there's Mary.

Along the street. Mary walking towards them, carrying messages.

JAMESIE. Wonder if she's missing a podger yet?

Andra and Dodie look at him.

(*Hurriedly, explaining himself.*) I mean that metaphorically speaking, boys! All's I mean's she might be feeling vulnerable, like! A bit insecure, know?

Mary passes.

JAMESIE. (*Calls.*) Yi awright there, Mary hen?

MARY. Aye.

JAMESIE. I'm just saying to my colleagues hen. Yi must be feeling a wee bit vulnerable like. With Rab being away. A wee tate insecure, know?

MARY. Aye. And I'll tell yi something else an' all.

JAMESIE. What's that?

MARY. (*Passing.*) I'm no half missing a podger . . .

Jamesie, Andra and Dodie look at each other. Burney stands, regarding them, sneering.

JAMESIE. Whit you looking at?

BURNEY. (*Innocently.*) Me, I never says a word.

He takes something from a message bag, chucks it towards them. We see Jamesie pick up a large meaty bone at his feet.

JAMESIE. (*To Andra and Dodie, bone in hand.*) He's his faither's son that yin awright . . .

Sound of Burney making barking noise.

JAMESIE. (*Mutters.*) Wee bastard!

SCENE 15. Inside the police station. Day.
Close-up on a 'Wanted' poster. 'Have You Seen This Man?' It shows a mug shot of Nesbitt, holding board displaying his prisoner number, his name prominent.

Nesbitt, sitting directly below the poster. He's in disguise, looks furtively self-conscious in shirt, tie, straw boater, dark glasses. He pulls the brim of the hat down further to obscure his bandage. A desk sergeant is dealing with someone at the desk. A few people sit near Nesbitt, awaiting attention.

NESBITT. (*Calls, to sergeant.*) Hey, Jim, any danger of getting served in here, by the way? My boy's done a bunk!

Offski

DESK SERGEANT. Just wait your turn! This isn't a supermarket . . .

NESBITT. (*Generally, to other people.*) Just wait my turn, eh? Christ, thae words'll be on my tombstone, boy, I'm telling yi . . . (*To man waiting.*) And they'll be on yours too if yi don't get that sneer off your fizzer pronto!

Man gets the sneer off his fizzer pronto.

Christ, gie a dog a bad name, eh? Just coz we're fae Glasgow yi think we're all bliddy mental or something! Well thae days is gone, boy, gone! See us, we're City of Culture, by the way. See me, I'm not just a punter anymore. I'm a *Euro Punter*! Refined, sophisticated and the epitome of innate good breeding. (*Gestures.*) So suck that, the lot of yeez!

DESK SERGEANT. (*Bellows.*) Next!

NESBITT. (*To others.*) Hey, yeez want to get a muzzle put on that dug, that's terrible. Where's the desk sergeant?

DESK SERGEANT. *I'm* the desk sergeant! What do you want?

NESBITT. (*At desk.*) What do I want? I'll have a wee bit of civility for a start, Rover! I'm in here trying to put a bit of business your way. I mean maybes crime doesn't pay, but you'd be a bliddy sight poorer withoot it, widn't yi!

DESK SERGEANT. Okay, let's start again. How can I help you?

NESBITT. That's better . . . (*Emotional.*) Yi can help iz fun my wean!

DESK SERGEANT. (*Baffled.*) Fun your wean?

NESBITT. Aye, it's my Gash. He's ran away from hame. His mother's at her wits end with worry, so she is! Honest to Christ, she'll be pisht oot her skull with anxiety, so she will!

DESK SERGEANT. I see. (*Getting a form.*) Well we better get a few details down then, shall we?

NESBITT. (*Wary.*) Details? What kinna details?

DESK SERGEANT. Well, we'll need to know his name for a start.

NESBITT. It's Gash! I telt yi, it's Gash!

DESK SERGEANT. His *full* name.

NESBITT. His full name? Oh I see, I see . . . (*Glances, worried over at poster.*) It's Gash Nnn . . .

DESK SERGEANT. Nn . . . ?

NESBITT. Aye, Nn . . . ! Two N's! It's Gaelic, know! Rob Roy and that, know! (*Sings nervously, glancing at poster.*) 'That old Scotch mither of mine . . .' Natural sense of rhythm, eh? Born right in us!

DESK SERGEANT. Fair enough. (*Makes note.*) Gash Nn . . . And what's your home address, Mr Nn?

NESBITT. My home address? It's *him* that's done the runner!

DESK SERGEANT. Yes, but I'm assuming your son still lives with you. He does still live with you, doesn't he?

NESBITT. Certainly he lives with me! But there's nothing in it! We're just good friends! What are you trying to insinuate, by the way?!

DESK SERGEANT. I'm not insinuating anything. I'm just trying to get some background.

NESBITT. Background is it? Christ, first it's details now it's background! I thought in the south yeez kept yourselves to yourselves? Christ, I came doon here hoping to get myself patronized a wee bit, know – Hullo Jock, here's ten pence get yourself a decent accent – not too much, just enough to keep the old chip on the shooder warm, know? But Christ Almighty next thing yi know they're wanting the story of yir life! (*To others.*) Whit youse gawping at? Bugger aff . . . !

DESK SERGEANT. (*Getting angry.*) Look you! Do you want us to help you or don't you?

NESBITT. No, no, don't put yourselves to any trouble on my account! I'm nothing, by the way, I'm nothing! Till there's another bliddy war, then yeez'll be creeping roon my house like damp up a wall! You'll be hearing from my solicitor. (*Pointing to straw hat.*) Just as soon as I get back from the Henley Regatta, there y'are! (*Turning away.*) Don't talk to me, don't talk to me!

DESK SERGEANT. Suit yourself . . .

Nesbitt walks a couple of paces, then to audience.

Offski

NESBITT. (*To sneering man.*) Hey, pal. Where is Henley and what the hell's a regatta, by the way?

The man opens his mouth to speak. Nesbitt clamps his hand over the man's mouth.

On second thoughts don't tell me! Anybody that'd know the answers to crap like that's too bliddy well boring to talk to! (*To audience, at door.*) Allow me, eh? I'm fair running amok with the social skills in't I?

He's at the door. He glances back to see the desk sergeant now standing in front of the desk looking quizzically at the poster on the wall.

NESBITT. (*Clocking him doing it.*) Oh Christ! (*To audience.*) That's the art of being a good guest, know? Aye knowing the right time to leave . . . !

He legs it out of the door.

Meanwhile the desk sergeant is finishing off drawing dark glasses and a boater on the poster. He regards the finished work for a moment then . . .

DESK SERGEANT. (*Shouting at door.*) Hey! Hey!

SCENE 16. The Nesbitts' living room. Day.
Mary on phone. She's anxious. Empty beer tins, full ashtrays.

MARY. Hullo, Rab? Rab? Where is he, have yi found him yet?

SCENE 17. Phone box. Day.
London (near South Bank). Nesbitt in phone box. (Minus dark glasses, boater etc.)

NESBITT. (*On phone.*) I'm trying, by the way, I'm bliddy trying! But it's a bliddy big place doon here, know!

Phoebe, sitting in a car outside parked on yellow lines, toots the horn impatiently.

Shouts at Phoebe, exasperated.

Awright, I'm coming, I'm coming!

A girl with a baby pokes her head round the door.

GIRL. Excuse me, but have you any spare change to get the baby . . .

133

This is one of me on irony patrol. Millions spent on this effort and all the time four hunner people are living underneath it in cardboard boxes. Should just pull up a chair and watch them. Much better story.

NESBITT. (*Exploding, exasperated.*) No I huvnie got bugger all change for the baby! (*Shouts into phone.*) I'll ring yi when I've fun him!

Slams down phone, exits from phone box, rounds on girl.

And I'll tell yi this, Miss Hollywood bliddy pathos . . .

Toot from Phoebe.

(*Jumping up and down.*) Awright, I'm coming. Bliddy kerb crawlers, you're all the same! (*To girl.*) That's a bliddy disgrace the way you people use your weans! See if you were a daughter of mine I'd tan your arse for yi! That's nothing but moral bliddy blackmail, that's all that is! And I'll tell yi something else . . .

GIRL. What's that?

NESBITT. It's a bliddy good sales pitch an all! (*Proffering,*

emotional.) Here, here ten bob, away and get it a bag of chips for
Christ's sake . . .

GIRL. (*Turning to go.*) Thanks very much . . .

NESBITT. (*After her.*) Hey doll . . .

She turns back.

I know it's a long shot. But I don't suppose *you've* come across a
wee Scots boy – no job, sleeping rough, bomber jacket and
trainers, have yi?

GIRL. Well, yes. As a matter of fact I have.

NESBITT. Yi have? Where?

GIRL. Not far from here. C'mon, I'll show you . . .

NESBITT. (*At car, to Phoebe.*) Hey you! Yi still looking for
business? (*Climbing in.*) Mon well, I'll show yi a good time . . . !

Phoebe slinks down behind the wheel, mortified.

SCENE 18. The Nesbitts' living room. Evening.
Burney lies on the settee, smoking, reading a DSS pamphlet.

Soft lights, music plays. We note the mood then cut to –

*The living room door. It's ajar, Jamesie pokes his head round. He looks
slicked up, smart. He sports a sleazy smile.*

JAMESIE. (*To Burney.*) Hullorerr, son. Yi awright.

BURNEY. In the pink. Yourself?

JAMESIE. No' bad, no' bad. (*Enters, concealing a bunch of flowers.*)
The door was off its hinges, so I just let myself in, know?

BURNEY. Feel free . . .

JAMESIE. (*Casually.*) So listen, eh, is your Mammy in, son?

BURNEY. Is she in? In what, Uncle Jamesie? In the nude?

JAMESIE. In the nude! Listen to him, wee scallywag! No, no, I
meant is your Mammy – available – I mean when I say available,
I mean . . .

BURNEY. She's available for you.

JAMESIE. Eh?

See the look in that wean's eyes? He's got soul. He better get rid of that pronto or he'll be another walking head wound afore too long.

BURNEY. She's in for you awright.

JAMESIE. She is?

BURNEY. Oh aye. In fact that's what she says. She says if your Uncle Jamesie slips roon, tell him I'm available. Whatever that means.

JAMESIE. She did?

BURNEY. Aye. What's with the flooers, Uncle Jamesie? Somebody deid?

JAMESIE. (*Awkward.*) Nah, nah, these isnae flooers, son! These is vegetables! Just gonny make a pan of soup, know? So, eh, where is your Mammy then, son?

BURNEY. She's in the bedroom. You're to go right up.

JAMESIE. (*Taken aback.*) Whut?

BURNEY. That's what she says, Uncle Jamesie. Tell your Uncle Jamesie he's to go right up. (*Points up at door.*) Just go right up.

JAMESIE. (*Swallows.*) I will, son. I will . . .

Exits.

Offski

SCENE 19. The Nesbitts' house, outside the bedroom door.
Evening.
Moments later.

Outside bedroom door. Jamesie's hand on the doorknob.

JAMESIE. (*Outside door.*) Mary! Mary darling, it's me. Snake hips
Cotter. No need to open the door. I'll just slither under the gap.

He opens the bedroom door.

Jamesie enters, turns on the light.

He looks to the bed. Nothing. He looks up.

*Dodie and Andra stand, also slicked up, also carrying bunches of
flowers, looking foolish.*

ANDRA. Hullo, Jamesie.

DODIE. Hiya, Jamesie. The nights are fair drawing in, in't they?

The door slams shut. A key turns in the lock.

BURNEY. (*From other side of the door.*) Hey boys!

ALL. What?

BURNEY. (*From other side.*) My Mammy canny come. But she
says to gie yeez this.

He slides something under the door. Andra picks it up.

DODIE. Whit is it?

ANDRA. A durty book!

BURNEY. (*From other side.*) And this.

Something else is slid under the door.

JAMESIE. What's that?

ANDRA. A box of Kleenex.

JAMESIE. (*Takes a deep breath.*) Right boys! There's only one thing
for it. (*He spits on palm.*) This never happened. Agreed?

*Andra and Dodie look at each other. They spit on their palms. They all
press palms together.*

ALL. (*Doing so.*) Agreed . . . !

137

Look at that! I've been years on the council list waiting for a hoose with a patio like that!

SCENE 20. 'Cardboard City'. Day.
London. 'Cardboard City' on the South Bank under Waterloo Bridge. The girl with the baby and Nesbitt on the concrete piazza, near the 'homes'. Phoebe bringing up the rear.

NESBITT. Is that it well? Is this us?

GIRL. Yes, this is it.

NESBITT. And are yi sure he's here? Wee Scots boy, no job, bomber jacket and trainers?

GIRL. Sure, I'm sure. Look. (*Indicates with a sweep of the arm.*) Take your pick from hundreds!

PHOEBE. Are all these people sleeping rough?

NESBITT. Nan, nah. They're queuing for tickets for the National Theatre.

He indicates an Old Vic theatre poster.

(*To audience.*) Look at that, eh? 'A Flea in Her Ear' be buggered. It's an ice pick through the brain some of them want doon here.

(*To Phoebe, scratching himself.*) 'Mon you . . . !

PHOEBE. (*Hurrying after him.*) Where are we going now?

NESBITT. Away to see a wee burd I know. See if she can pull a few strings for me kinna style, know?

PHOEBE. 'Wee burd'? What 'wee burd'?

SCENE 21. Outside.
Same day. Later.

Nesbitt is walking along, talking to someone. We don't yet see who.

NESBITT. Whit'd yi mean, whit'd yi mean she'll no' see me? Listen, me and her's right good mates. We had a wee natter last year when she came to open the drying oot ward in the Southern General!

No response.

Christ you're a right stand-offish bugger in't yi . . . ?

We pull out to show a guardsman in bearskin marching up and down outside the gates of Buckingham Palace. Nesbitt has been addressing him.

Christ sake, all's I want's a wee amnesty offa the monarch, know. So's I can get the filth to look for my boy!

A policeman stands.

No offence, Jim. Present company excepted, know . . .

PHOEBE. (*Standing nearby.*) I told you this was pointless!

NESBITT. Look lady, is it not time for your change of life or something? When I want your advice, I'll get my heid examined, right? Until then, I'll handle this my way, I'll handle this the Rab C. Nesbitt way! I'll handle this . . .

PHOEBE. The wrong way.

NESBITT. Look, you're too sophisticated for a skite across the chops, yi know! Noo gawn, get oot my sight, I've some diplomatic overtures to make here!

Moves off.

POLICEMAN. (*To Phoebe.*) Is that man bothering you, madam?

PHOEBE. Him? No. He's only a danger to himself, that one.

A shout is heard. Nesbitt is calling up to the Palace windows.

NESBITT. (*Shouts.*) Lizzie . . . ! (*Sing-song.*) Liz-zie Wind-sorrr! Gonny chuck iz down a royal par-do-on . . . ? (*To audience.*) There y'are, eh? Who says I'm not a yuppy? Christ, the last time I shouted up at a windae my Maw flung iz doon a piece on treacle.

Policeman appears, prods Nesbitt along, roughly.

POLICEMAN. Right you, that's enough! On your way . . . !

NESBITT. Awright, keep the heid, what yi prodding at? Think it's a bliddy sheep yi got there or something. Christ, the highland clearances is finished boy! (*Rubbing his arm.*) Finito . . . !

POLICEMAN. On your way, Jock. Before you get into trouble.

NESBITT. Oh, it's Jock noo is it? Wee bit of friendly racism, eh? That's what I like aboot you polis doon here, you've got a face for every occasion. Christ, if I was a yank tae, yi'd be giving it (*doing one*) the George Dixon knee bends and offering me a shot of yir helmet!

POLICEMAN. I'm warning you.

NESBITT. Awright, awright. Hey, did I not see you at the Notting Hill Carnival by the way. Was that not you with the yam doon yir troosers limbo dancing under a joint? (*Moving sharpish.*) Awright, I'm gawn, I'm gawn! (*To Phoebe.*) 'Mon you . . . !

PHOEBE. (*Hurrying behind.*) Where are we going now?

NESBITT. Well I've tried the top, and I've tried the bottom. So I might as well scrape under the barrel noo . . .

SCENE 22. Downing Street. Day.
Same day. A little later.

A policeman stands outside number Ten. Nesbitt approaches him. Tries to enter the building. The policeman gives a dubious look.

NESBITT. (*To policeman.*) Yi awright there, pal? Is the government in? It's okay, I'm fae number nine. Just nicking in to collect their catalogue money, know . . .

The policeman extends a hand, stopping him.

Offski

Oh hey, hey, what's the gemme. Rab C. Nesbitt, Ambassador for Govan, by the way! Diplomatic immunity and that, know.

Tries to get in the other side. Policeman stretches out his other hand, stopping him. Nesbitt gives up.

NESBITT. Ach, awright. Well gonny gie her this well? (*Hands something to the policeman.*) It's okay, it's not a petition. It's just an eviction notice, wrut on a dod of Andrex, but believe me, it comes from the heart of a nation!

Policeman screws up the paper, lets it drop.

(*To audience.*) So much for the will of the people, eh? (*Push from policeman.*) Awright, I'm gawn, I'm gawn . . . ! (*Shouts back.*) Hey, I don't want to spoil your day nor nothing. But there's been a press leak. They're starting a neighbourhood watch scheme roon here. You've to get made redundant! Tube! (*To Phoebe, who stands, po-faced.*) What you looking at?

PHOEBE. Are they all like you in Scotland?

NESBITT. Nah, nah, some of them's aggressive. (*Pushing her.*) Noo come on! Get your arse in gear and gie's a hurl back to wur billet!

SUBTITLE. May I have a lift home please?

PHOEBE. No I will not 'get my arse in gear', Rab C. Nesbitt, or whatever it is you call yourself! I've had enough of you!

Startled look from Nesbitt.

If you want a lift, you will ask me in a civilised manner! You will ask me in an English manner!

NESBITT. Whit'd yi mean, whit'd yi mean?

PHOEBE. You will say, 'Phoebe, I would be awfully grateful if you would kindly oblige me with a lift to Sidcup please.'

NESBITT. Away to . . .

PHOEBE. Suit yourself! Otherwise you can walk to Sidcup!

NESBITT. (*After an inner struggle.*) Awright, awright! Phoebe . . .

PHOEBE. Yes?

NESBITT. I would be awfully grateful . . . If you would kindly oblige me . . . (*Blurts it out.*) with a bliddy well lift to Sidcup!

PHOEBE. Tally ho pip pip.

NESBITT. (*On verge of exploding.*) Tally ho, bliddy well pip pip.

PHOEBE. And God bless Margaret Thatcher.

NESBITT. (*A moment's quivering restraint, then erupts.*) Get to! Get oot my bliddy sight! Yi can stick your lift! I don't want it! (*Aiming a kick.*) Gawn!

Phoebe squeals, legs it.

I will bliddy well walk, by the way! You'll not civilise me, lady! I'll be a lounge lizard for nobody! Nobody! (*To audience, rage spent.*) Awright, fair enough, so I made an arse of myself. But at least I done it for Scotland . . . ! (*Clenched fist, then walks.*)

SCENE 23. Shug's living room. Evening.
Shug stands, fondling his putter. Phoebe enters, pushing hostess trolley.

SHUG. Walked. What'd you mean walked?

PHOEBE. I mean put one foot in front of the other. It is the easiest way to do it, Hugh. (*Puts some dishes on a coffee table.*)

SHUG. But the man's a guest in our house. You don't abuse your house guests, Phoebe. It's not on. I mean come to grips.

PHOEBE. 'Not on'? 'Come to grips'? Hugh. Do I detect a hint of the vernacular here?

SHUG. You detect more than a bliddy hint, lady. You detect the whole shebang and no mistake!

PHOEBE. Oh it's all coming out now, isn't it? All the rottenness! All the bile! Accrued from a lifetime of guzzling baked beans in tenements!

SHUG. Oh I see. So the mittens are off now, are they? We're hitting below the angora line. (*Nesbittish.*) Well I will tell you this lady. Tenements is it? They might have slums on the outside. But there were hearts of gold pulsing on the inside! My mother went doon on her bended knees and she cleaned stairs! Stairs! So that I could get a decent education!

PHOEBE. That must have been a convenient posture for you, Hugh.

SHUG. Whit'd yi mean?

PHOEBE. It made it easier for you to walk all over her.

SHUG. Ya dirty wee thin-lipped midden! Yi think yir so bliddy well superior, don't yi, eh!

PHOEBE. Yes. But only compared to you.

SHUG. (*Frustrated.*) See you . . . ! See you . . . ! You're . . . !

Cuckoo clock strikes once.

SHUG. (*To clock.*) Right ya wee twee bass yi, you're claimed!

He gives a wild cry, takes a swing at the clock with the putter.

SHUG. There y'are, lady! Did yi see that, eh? Did yi see that! Break out the strait jackets! (*Punching the air.*) Big mad mental Shug from Polmadie is back!

PHOEBE. It's not a strait jacket you need. It's a bib and rompers. Where are you going?

SHUG. (*At door.*) Out to look efter me and mines! Oot to reclaim my birthright!

PHOEBE. (*To audience.*) They're a sad race really. I blame the diet. I mean only two sorts of people eat porridge. Convicts . . . and Scotsmen.

Door slams. Vibration shakes cuckoo clock off the wall. It falls, giving a sad squawk.

SCENE 24. Westminster Bridge. Evening.
We see Big Ben large in the foreground. Nesbitt walking near it over bridge.

NESBITT. (*Shouting to left and right.*) Gash! Gash! Bliddy place this is, by the way. (*Indicating to Big Ben.*) Look at that durty big effort there tae. The Big Ben, boy. Standing there flashing itself, giving it laldy with the pomp and circumstance. I canny get away with all thon stuff me. All thon Dunkirk spirit. I mean what is thon all aboot, eh? Christ. We got stiffened tae, we got massacred at Dunkirk, boy! Big Adolf drove us into the sea! Christ sake, if you ask me that's how all the holiday beaches is so polluted noo, it's fae all us Brits crapping ourselves at Dunkirk! But there y'are, eh. Maybes you can work it oot, I'm just simple

For a balanced analysis, over now to
our political correspondent Rant C. Nesbitt.

scum, know? (*Shouts.*) Gash! Gash!

Big Ben strikes.

All the same, I'll say this for that big bugger . . .

Strikes again.

He's got some size of dong on him, hin't he, eh? (*Resumes shouting.*) Gash! Gash son, where are yi . . . ?

SCENE 25. The Nesbitts' living room. Evening.
Mary sitting at phone distraught, cradling a picture of Gash and Nesbitt. She sniffs noisily, wipes away a tear. Burney, on the settee, regards her.

BURNEY. (*Calls.*) Haw, Maw!

MARY. Whit!

BURNEY. Listen, is it not aboot time you screwed the bobbin here?

MARY. Whit'd yi mean?

BURNEY. It's time you remembered you've got two weans and not just one. I mean see all this neglect, it could be stunting my emotional growth, yi know.

MARY. Yi know son, maybe you're right. Maybe I have got things oot of proportion. But you know there's no favourite in my hoose. (*Puts down picture, advances open-armed.*) C'mere son, and gie your mammy a nice big . . .

BURNEY. (*Fending her off instantly.*) Get away tae! Geeza brek! Bugger aff!

MARY. (*Hurt.*) But son, I thought yi wanted . . .

BURNEY. (*Reclining, picking up a Viz*) Ya kidding? I was just checking. Now away and get milked . . .

Settles back with comic, gets skite across head.

Aya . . . !

MARY. (*Tearful, looking at photo.*) Gash . . . !

SCENE 26. Shug's house. Evening.
Later. Gash, sitting huddled in a blanket, looking unkempt, bleary-eyed. Shug proffers him a mug of tea which Gash accepts, gratefully.

GASH. Thanks, Uncle Hugh! I'll never forget yi for this! Yi musta pulled some amount of strings to get them to find me.

SHUG. Call me, Shug, son. And that's what strings are for. (*Ruffing Gash's hair.*) After all, us trash've got to stick tegither, hin't we eh?

PHOEBE. (*Sitting, knitting.*) Yes, bonded by ringworm. How very Celtic of you.

SHUG. She's English son. They're a queer race. That'll be her crotcheting a purse to keep her ovaries in.

PHOEBE. I just don't see what all this fuss is about!

A ring at the doorbell. Excitement.

SHUG. That'll be him! Your Da's here, son! (*Calls towards kitchen.*) Are yeez right in there?

GASH. (*From offstage.*) Yes!

SHUG. (*To Gash, enthused.*) I canny wait to see his fizzer when you open that door!

Trusting smile from Gash.

SCENE 27. Outside front door of Shug's house. Evening.
Nesbitt stands, looking tired, disconsolate. An unmarked van is parked in the street.

NESBITT. (*To audience.*) What's it all about, eh? Yi bring them into the world. Yi embarrass them, yi beat them insensible. Yi do your best to gie them a lousy childhood so they'll grow up with an inferiority complex and at least have something to build on in later life. And how do they repay yi for all that sacrifice? They sling their hook! (*Shouts to man in van.*) Yi got weans yirself, Jim?

The man in the van, in hat, overcoat, head down, ignores him.

(*To audience.*) I'll tell yi this though. I'd gie a year's Family Credit to see the plooky wee fizzog of his again!

He turns to face the door. Gash stands, smiling.

GASH. Da.

NESBITT. Gash!

GASH. (*With arms outstretched.*) Da . . . !

NESBITT. (*Draws back a fist to throw a punch.*) Gash! Ya durty wee . . . ! (*Settles for a clip round the ear.*) Ya wee messin yi! How the hell'd you get here?

GASH. I was dead jammy, Da. It was Uncle Shuggy. He used his connections with the local filth.

NESBITT. What connections?

Shug appears, beaming.

SHUG. Like I always say, Rab. It's amazing what yi can achieve with a masonic handshake and an ingratiating manner. Meet Sergeant Grover . . .

The desk sergeant from earlier appears in the doorway with Shug. A policeman behind him.

SERGEANT. Rab C. Nesbitt?

NESBITT. (*Clocking him.*) Oh Christ . . .

SHUG. It was a doddle, Rab. I just nipped down the station, told the Sergeant all about yeez and he was only too happy to get the Met to scour the doss holes for the boy. (*Proffering hand.*) Me and you share the same lodge, don't we, Brother?

DESK SERGEANT. (*Ignoring hand.*) Don't get cocky, Jock. We only needed a spot of tokenism for appearances sake. And you were the whitest wog we could dredge up. (*To Nesbitt.*) We've been looking for you, Nesbitt. Get inside.

The Scottish policemen from earlier leap from the unmarked van.

FIRST POLICEMAN. (*Halfway up path.*) He's not going anywhere. Except back up the road with us!

NESBITT. (*To Scottish policeman.*) Oh hullorerr! (*To audience.*) Christ, it's nice to be popular, in't it?

FIRST POLICEMAN. He's wanted on sixteen charges of non-payment of fines. All committed in Glasgow!

DESK SERGEANT. Well, they might have been committed in Glasgow. But he was apprehended in Sidcup. This is our collar. If you want him, you'll have to go through the appropriate channels.

NESBITT. This'll take a wee bit of time. Why don't I slope off for a wee game of cricket or something . . .

FIRST POLICEMAN. (*Seizing Nesbitt's collar.*) Shuttit you! (*To desk sergeant.*) Look Jim, we huvnie time to argue, right? So I'm taking him in on channel STPWE, okay?

DESK SERGEANT. And what, pray, is channel STPWE?

FIRST POLICEMAN. (*Nutting him.*) Stitch That Pal, We're Offski . . . ! Mon . . .

Desk sergeant drops, moaning. Shug grabs Nesbitt by the lapel.

SHUG. Look, Rab. Just what is going on here! I'm entitled to some kind of explanation!

NESBITT. No offence, Shug. But see next time you want to lend a helping hand?

SHUG. Yes?

NESBITT. (*Nutting him.*) Just stick your foot in your gub first, okay? (*To Second Policeman.*) Awright, quick, get it ower with.

Second Policeman hits him over the head with a truncheon.

NESBITT. (*Dropping.*) Cheers, awrabest.

Phoebe appears in the doorway, surveys the scene. Desk sergeant and Shug lie bleeding, moaning. Nesbitt is being borne away by two Scots policemen.

PHOEBE. I was about to ask if you'd all care for a pot of tea?

GASH. (*Down the path.*) No thanks, Auntie Phoebe. We're offski . . . !

PHOEBE. Oh all right. Well 'Haste Ye Back'. (*Mutters.*) But not too soon I hope . . .

Shug groans.

PHOEBE. Hugh! For goodness sake stop moaning. The neighbours will think you're drunk!

She gives him a vicious little kick as he lies there.

SHUG. Sorry, my dove . . .

PHOEBE. (*In a hiss.*) Don't be sorry, be careful . . . ! (*She turns, waves a pleasant goodbye, cardy over shoulders.*) 'Bye . . . !

SCENE 28. Exterior Glasgow Central Station concourse. Day.
Jamesie, Andra and Dodie sit, drinking, eating burgers. Nesbitt passes, on a stretcher, being carried by two policemen.

JAMESIE. (*To others.*) Hey look, boys, there's Rab. (*Calls.*) Hey Rab, how'd yi get on in London?

NESBITT. (*Sitting up.*) Och, yi know what they say, Jamesie. It's awright for a fracture, but I widnae like to be terminal there, know?

He clocks Burney, bag in hand, walking across the concourse.

(*Calls.*) Haw! Wee yin! What'd yi think you're doing?

BURNEY. Whit'd yi think I'm doing? I'm running away. That's the only way yi get any attention roon here!

GASH. (*To Burney.*) Hey, Tom Sawyer! (*Tugging his own.*) Want a lend of my petted lip?

BURNEY. Shuttit you. Just wait to my Maw fun's oot I'm missing. You'll no half see the bitch running.

Mary coming running along the concourse, shouting.

MARY. (*Shouting.*) Burney! Here! Wait!

BURNEY. (*Innocently, with superior look to Gash.*) Aye Mammy, what is it?

Some clothing hits him in the face.

MARY. If you're gawn, take your manky washing with yi. It's not a hotel I'm running! (*To Gash, hugging him.*) Hullo, son. It's lovely to have yi back again!

GASH. It's lovely to be back, Mammy . . .

Burney and Gash exchange 'V' signs behind Mary's back as Gash and Mary walk away, hugging.

BURNEY. (*Chucking down his bag.*) Ach, sod this. (*Calls.*) Hey, Cotter! Gee's a swig out that bottle . . . !

Jamesie gives him the bottle.

BURNEY. (*To audience.*) Tell yi one thing about up here. At least we've got a sense of community. (*Takes a swig.*) Nae brain cells of course, just a poxy sense of community!

JAMESIE. (*To Burney.*) You're staying, eh son? Good thing too! There's no place like Scotland!

BURNEY. It's nae more than we deserve, boss. (*To others.*) Okay, let's gie it laldy with the National Anthem! (*Leading them off.*) 'Oh, flower of Scotland . . .'

They all sway about, singing. Much stomping of feet.

Further along concourse. Nesbitt sits up dazedly on the stretcher, bottle of beer in hand.

NESBITT. (*To audience.*) Did yi see that, eh? Did yi see that? Wha's like us, eh . . . ? Wha's like us . . . ?

He sticks the bottle into his ear, removes top, holds up bottle.

Slange . . . ! (*Drinks.*)

Rab C. Nesbitt

EPISODE SIX

City of Culture

CAST LIST

LORD PROVOST	John Bett
JOHN, HIS ASSISTANT	Freddie Boardley
RAB C. NESBITT	Gregor Fisher
SENIOR POLICE INSPECTOR	James Cosmo
LEAD FRENCH DIGNITARY	Dave Anderson
WOMAN FRENCH DIGNITARY	Vicki Burton
BURNEY	Eric Cullen
GASH	Andrew Fairlie
AMERICAN WOMAN TOURIST	Lynn Ferguson
AMERICAN MAN TOURIST	William Armour
STREET VENDOR	Jack Milroy
JAMESIE COTTER	Tony Roper
PERUVIAN FOLK LEADER	Billy McElhanney
MARY NESBITT	Elaine C. Smith
ELLA COTTER	Barbara Rafferty
MAGISTRATE	Iain Cuthbertson
HOSPITAL RECEPTIONIST	Emma Currie
DOCTOR	Sandy Welch

City of Culture

SCENE 1. Glasgow. Day.
Montage of shots of Glasgow, e.g. Princes Square, George Square, St Enoch Centre, City Chambers etc.

Glasgow 1990 theme song.

SCENE 2. City Chambers. Day.
Front of the City Chambers. The Lord Provost and John, his assistant, stand before the main entrance.

LORD PROVOST. This is the gemme, eh John? City of Culture! In't it great to be an aesthete?

JOHN. Pure brand new, Boss. Here, gimme five!

They slap skin.

BOTH. (*revelling in it.*) Hull-ooo!

PROVOST. So listen, tell me, are the preparations made?

JOHN. Aye, Provost, for the thousandth time!

PROVOST. (*Glancing anxiously up and down.*) And what time are the French arriving?

JOHN. Any minute now. Whatever Paris did in '89, we'll do better in 1990! We'll show them the sleek new upmarket Glasgow, eh Provost.

PROVOST. Certainmont!

Nesbitt appears, crawling. He tugs at the Provost's trouser leg.

NESBITT. Hey pal. Haw.

PROVOST. (*Gives a little yap of horror.*) In the name of God, John, look what's crawling up my leg!

NESBITT. Hey, pal, where's the culture? I'm trying to get oot to the Burrell collection, know? See the Burrells. Gonny lend iz ten pence for my bus fare?

PROVOST. (*Struggling to free himself*) Do something, John!

JOHN. Bloody low life. We can't get rid of them, Provost. They keep creeping out from under the floorboards. (*Shooing.*) Go on you, shoo! Get lost!

NESBITT. What'd yi mean 'get lost'? I live here by the way.

PROVOST. For God's sake do something, John! Here come the Paris delegation now!

Limo, some distance off, approaching.

JOHN. (*Panicking.*) What'll I do with it?

NESBITT. Is it a song yeez are wanting? Nae bother. (*Singing.*) 'Oh, Las Vegas, you'll be the death of me . . .

PROVOST. Anything! (*Noticing an open drain.*) Look, stuff him down that stank there!

JOHN. Right, Provost.

PROVOST. And where the hell's all the drain covers gone in this city by the way?

JOHN. How should I know? Drain covers arnie my brief. (*Grabbing Nesbitt by the scruff.*) 'Mon you.

NESBITT. Haw, haw, keep the heid . . .

PROVOST. What'd you mean they're not your brief?

JOHN. I'm welfare, aren't I? I'm health and social concern! (*To Nesbitt*) C'mon you. Get down that bloody sewer where you came from!

NESBITT. Who'd you think you're talking to, boy? You looking for a whap on the melt? Coz I'm just the active citizen to give yi one!

PROVOST. (*Pulling John.*) Easy, John! Don't startle him. You know what they say, one swipe from a bear's paw can break your leg!

JOHN. (*Shrinking back.*) Right, Provost . . .

NESBITT. What'd yi mean 'bear' by the way? I'm getting steamed into the culture, boy! I'm gawn to meet my mate Jamesie Cotter then we're going oot to steep wurselves in art, there y'are!

JOHN. (*To Provost.*) Steep himself in Dettol might be better.

NESBITT. (*Pointing.*) See you, toe-rag, you're exploiting my good nature, so yi are!

The Provost and John cling to one another. A senior police inspector

Top: Win £££s in our 'Spot the Scumball' competition.
Bottom: Glasgow Smiles Better.

appears, in uniform, singing.

SENIOR POLICEMAN. (*Singing.*) 'Glas-gow smiles bet . . . *(Breaks off.)* Afternoon, gentlemen, everything alright?

NESBITT. Aye, no' bad pal. How's yirself?

SENIOR POLICEMAN. Shuttit you.

PROVOST. It would be, Alastair. But we're getting a wee tate of agitation offa Biffo here.

SENIOR POLICEMAN. That a fact. Well, he's not too old for a clip around the ear.

NESBITT. That's the gemme, pal! You tell them. That's fighting talk just like the old days!

SENIOR POLICEMAN. Hardly. (*Calls over Nesbitt's shoulder.*) Constable! Give this yin a clip around the ear!

CONSTABLE. Right, sir.

The Constable, standing behind Nesbitt, attaches a clip to Nesbitt's ear.

SENIOR POLICEMAN. (*To Provost.*) Of course nowadays it's a crocodile clip but the principle's just the same.

CONSTABLE. Alright, Judy.

A policewoman, holding a small black box, presses a button discharging an electric impulse. Nesbitt yells, leaps in pain..

NESBITT. Aya! Durty masonic big ... (*Dazed.*) In the namea ...

SENIOR POLICEMAN. (*To Provost.*) Pretty gallus, eh, Provost? And the very top of the range in designer state violence, I'm reliably informed.

PROVOST. D'you hear that, John? Soon we'll be right up there with Nicaragua!

JOHN AND PROVOST. (*Slapping skin.*) Hull-ooo!

Limo has pulled up. Some dignitaries get out. The leading dignitary speaks.

LEAD DIGNITARY. Pardon us. But is this the City of Culture?

PROVOST. You bet your sweet arse it is, pal! (*Full of himself.*) John, take wur guests up the John Knox Suite for a spritzer!

(*A young woman French Dignitary almost puts her foot down the open drain, gives a little startled yell. John seizes her by the elbow.*)

JOHN. Easy, mon cherie!

WOMAN DIGNITARY. But how strange. Why are there no drain covers?

JOHN. (*Bluffing.*) Och, it's the City of Culture, doll, they were the wrong shade, so we sent them back.

WOMAN DIGNITARY. Sent them back?

JOHN. Yes. We wanted something in cerise, to blend with all the red sandstone, know?

Over woman Dignitary's shoulder he clocks Nesbitt. He shoos him away with his hand, unseen to woman Dignitary.

JOHN. Beat it you! Shoo!

NESBITT. (*Shouts back.*) Aye, I'm gawn! I'm gawn . . . !

SCENE 3. City Street. Day.
Same Day. Same Time. A banner is strung across the street. It proclaims 'Glasgow City of Culture'.

Music: Quick blast of 'Culture' song.

Pavement, below the banner, Gash is shouting down a drain. He holds a rope that is tied to the drain cover. A battered pram stands nearby.

GASH. (*Shouting down.*) Shove ya wee disease yi! Shove!

VOICE. (*From offstage*) I'm shoving! I'm shoving!

They strain. The drain cover gives. Gash yanks it from its setting.

Burney pokes his head up from down the drain, takes a look about.

BURNEY. Christ, what a dump. It's cleaner doon the sewers than it is in the streets, so it is.

GASH. (*Skites him.*) Shuttit you! Stop knocking Glasgow! Glesga's made us what we are today!

BURNEY. What are we today?

GASH. I'm not sure. But pamp on your urchin bunnet quick. Here comes a tourist.

Two American tourists, a man and a woman, approach.

GASH. (*Hand cupped.*) Hey Jim. City of Culture. Yi got ten pence for a cappocino?

MALE TOURIST. Pardon me?

WOMAN TOURIST. We're from the USA.

GASH. Is that right? We're fae Govan. That's my wee brar, Burney.

BURNEY. Howdy.

GASH. (*To woman.*) Just rubber ear him, doll, he's a tube. How yeez getting on with the lingo, by the way?

The couple look at each other, uncomprehending.

MALE TOURIST. Why is your brother down the drain?

GASH. Business, Jim. We've entered the entrepreneurial spirit of the new revitalised Glesga.

BURNEY. Aye. We knock the drain covers and flog them to McIntosh's scrap yard.

GASH. (*To Burney.*) Shuttit you. Who's doing the PR here?

WOMAN TOURIST. Well, we wish you every success.

BURNEY. Cheers, doll. Maybe someday we'll buy wur own cesspit, eh.

MALE TOURIST. (*Clenched fist salute.*) Go for it!

FEMALE TOURIST. (*Takes a quick pic of them.*) 'Bye!

GASH. (*To Burney.*) Nice race of people the yanks, eh? At least they treat yi as equals.

BURNEY. I'm not too sure about that.

GASH. How no'?

BURNEY. (*Picking something up.*) The bastards are flinging us peanuts.

The two tourists, chucking nuts.

Gash and Burney, making monkey noises and movements.

SCENE 4. City street. Day.
Same day, same time. Nesbitt walking along a city street.

NESBITT. Culture is it? Don't talk to me. See me? See culture? See Pavarotti? See the Japanese nose flute? See thon? (*He points to some paintings in the window of an art shop.*) Yi can stuff it, there y'are. I mean don't get me wrong. I revere mankind's highest achievements, I'm nae wallapur, know? But I mean, be fair, what's stuff like that got to do with keech like me, know? I like real art! I like punter art! Something with a wee taste of the old shite and onions to it, know?

He moves on a little. A street vendor is selling tatty junk from a stall. Tatty schmalzy prints abound.

NESBITT. (*To audience.*) Oho, eh? Now you're talking! See that Oscar Wilde, by the way? Big Oz had it wrong. He says all art is useless. But not punter art, boy. Punter art's strictly functional. See this keech here. (*He points to a crappy print of a small boy, looking up, crying.*) I mean, be honest, it's completely minging to look at. But it's just the job for hiding thon durty mark yi get above the gas fire in the living room, know? (*To vendor*) Awright there, pal? I was just saying (*Picking up a piece of rubbish.*) You've no half got some lovely examples of Govan folk art here, know?

VENDOR. (*Student.*) It's crap. All crap! I just give the public what they want. Man is a useless passion.

NESBITT. Well so what? I'm a useless bastard but I can still stick a smile on my fizzer from time totime. Gawn, get tae . . . ! (To audience.) See that yin? It's the likes of him that gets Glesga a bad name, so it is . . . . (*Accosts a passer by.*) Hey Jim, City of Culture. Gonny see iz ten pence for a fondue set? (*As passer by ignores him.*) Philistine!

SCENE 5. Pedestrian Precinct. Day.
Same day.

A group of Peruvian Folk Musicians, dressed as Aztecs, are playing pan pipes. A small crowd watches.

We find Jamesie Cotter at the back. He's draining a can.

A Passer by places the remnants of a fast food takeaway into a little bin by him. Jamesie has a look at it.

JAMESIE. (*Calls after passer by.*) Bliddy rubbitch! I don't know how yi can bring yirself to eat fast food!

A second passer by drips a bag of chips into the bin. Jamesie fishes it out.

JAMESIE. (*Calls after second passer by.*) That's more like it! (*Holds up a chip.*) Home cooking! (*Eating.*) Yi canny whack it, eh pal . . .

Nesbitt appears.

NESBITT. Jamesie! Jamesie!

157

**Straight up, Jamesie. If I had a spare
ticket for the Bolshoi Ballet, I'd gie you it.**

JAMESIE. Rab!

Loving embrace.

JAMESIE. Where the hell have yi been, Rab? We've got to get up
that Burrell collection. Meet wur spouses, know?

NESBITT. Aye, right!

They stand, swaying.

There's just one thing, Jamesie.

JAMESIE. What's that, Rab?

NESBITT. Where the hell is the Burrell collection?

JAMESIE. I don't know. I thought you knew.

NESBITT. Is it licensed like? Do they take bookies' lines?

JAMESIE. No.

NESBITT. Well how the hell would I know? Use your noddle. Far . . .

JAMESIE. Sorry, Rab, I wasnie thinking. Tell yi what. (*Indicating folk group.*) We'll ask these blokes, they're into art and that. They'll maybes know.

NESBITT. Aye right. 'Mon (*Pushing through crowd.*) 'Scuse us, doll. S'awright. We're ethnic, know.

JAMESIE. Aye. We're the McScum, clan, know. The tribe that hides from man!

NESBITT. Aye, the rent man! (*Laughs.*) Just a wee joke there, know! A wee jolly jape from Giro valley!

Sour faces.

NESBITT. Ach, well suit yirselfs . . . (*Calls.*) Hey, Jim! Pedro!

The Folk Group. They've stopped playing. The Folk leader is speaking, in halting English to the audience.

LEADER. Is good be here, Glasgow England. We come Peru. Thank you very glad . . .

NESBITT. (*To folk leader.*) Hey, pal! Haw! Where's the Burrell collection and that?

LEADER. Que?

NESBITT. El paintings! El arto!

JAMESIE. We're gawn to meet wur wifes! Wifes!

NESBITT. (*Grinding hips.*) El rumpy bumby, know?

(*Quizzical look from leader.*)

JAMESIE. Wur wasting wur time, Rab. This bloke's a spam case. Disnae understand a word.

NESBITT. That's not the attitude, Jamesie. These blokes is visitors. We need to strike up a rapport, know?

JAMESIE. Aye, fair enough . . .

NESBITT. Hey, pal. Whit yi chanting aboot? (*Very deliberately.*) El songo!

LEADER. Ah. I sing of my country. Of the high mountain. And of the shepherd who plays his pan pipes among the llama.

JAMESIE. Pipes, eh? Maybes he does requests, Rab! (*To leader.*) Hey pal, d'you know 'Blanket on the Ground'?

NESBITT. Aye! Tammy Wynette! She's fae America! That's just doon the road fae Peru!

LEADER. (*Wary.*) No. I sing only of the llama.

JAMESIE. Sod the bliddy llama! Gie's a decent belter by the way!

NESBITT. (*Enthusiastically.*) Something we can stomp wur feet tae! And get joining in the chorus!

JAMESIE. Aye!

The other Peruvians shout for Peruvian leader to hurry up.

LEADER. (*Shouts back.*) Si, I come! (*To Nesbitt and Jamesie.*) Look, see if youse pair don't bugger aff pronto, me and the other Aztecs is gonny take yi behind thae cut out Andes and gie yeez a pummelling that'll last to next culture year, understood!

NESBITT. Hey, that doesnie sound like Aztec talk to me. What the hell part of Peru are you fae?

LEADER. Paisley. But as far as you and the social security snoopers is concerned, I'm the bliddy Sun King, *okay*?

NESBITT. Oh hey, wait a minute pal. It's like that, is it, it's like that? Listen, you canny work in Glesga till yi get yir visa stamped!

LEADER. Oh aye. And where do I do that like?

JAMESIE. (*Nutting him*) Right here!

LEADER. Aya! (*Shouts.*) Get them boys! They're trying to mess with wur hustle!

PERUVIAN. (*Shouts.*) Mon, boys! Aztecs ya bass! Intae rum!

A fight ensues, which we only hear but don't see.

Cut to –

A little distance away. Mary and Ella have appeared. They look at the melee.

City of Culture

Top: **MUGGING HORROR!** Govan men gubbed by Aztecs.
Bottom: Yeez think yeez are smart bastards just coz yeez are a lost civilisation!

MARY. Would yi look at them, Ella. Drunk men fighting. What a terrible image to present of Glasgow.

ELLA. I know. Hanging's too good for them! They should lock them up and throw away the key, whoever they are!

The fight.

All concerned grappling, trousers scrunched up, bare calves visible. Grunting and shouting. Policemen appear, start nicking.

Jamesie, in a head lock, catches sight of Ella.

JAMESIE. Ella! Don't just stand there. Get up that Citizens' Advice Bureau and see about getting me Legal Aid!

Ella, mortified.

ELLA. (*Covering her face.*) In the namea . . . I'm mortified!

Nesbitt, on ground, arm up back, clocking Mary.

NESBITT. Mary, doll! Look on the bright side! At least for once I'm on time!

MARY. (*Shouts back.*) Aye, yi would've been! But yi were supposed to be here yesterday! (*To Ella.*) Come on, Ella, we'll nick up Littlewoods reshtrant. Have a moan aboot the price of the fruit scones.

ELLA. Right, Mary. I could just do with slagging an innocent counter assistant. (*Looking towards fight.*) Tubes . . . !

SCENE 6. Courtroom. Day.
Nesbitt and Jamesie in dock. A policeman in attendance.

Mary and Ella in public gallery.

MAGISTRATE. Rab C. Nesbitt?

NESBITT. The very same, boss. Awrabest . . .

MAGISTRATE. Silence! You will show this court respect! (*To Jamesie.*) James Aaron Cotter?

JAMESIE. That's me. Long live the King, by the way!

MAGISTRATE. (*Fiercely, banging gavel.*) I said respect! This is a courtroom, not a music hall, *understood?*

Nesbitt and Jamesie are taken aback.

MAGISTRATE. People like you are a disgrace to Glasgow, do you know that? Good God, we're the European City of Culture! The eyes of the world are upon us! Scum like you must be the equivalent of ten thousand lost civil servant jobs to this city. Does that mean nothing to either of you?

Nesbitt and Jamesie exchange a look.

Goering said that when he heard the word 'culture' he reached for his revolver. I wonder what you reach for Nesbitt, when you hear the word 'culture'?

JAMESIE. His dictionary, probably, am I right, Rab?

NESBITT. Oh I don't know Jamesie, what's a dictionary?

They share a laugh. Enraged banging of gavel.

NESBITT. (*To magistrate.*) Sorry boss, just a wee bit of scum banter there, know. (*Catching sight.*) Haw, Mary hen! Yi awright doll?

MARY. We'll awright youse when we get yeez hame, don't worry about that!

MAGISTRATE. Silence! This type of stereotypical drunken brawling has to cease! Filth must be kept off the streets!

JAMESIE. (*To policeman.*) I hope you're listening to this.

POLICEMAN. (*Giving him a skite.*) Shuttit you!

MAGISTRATE. Have you anything to say before I pass sentence?

NESBITT. Aye, I've got something to say. I would just like to know who the hell this city's being run for these days! For them that lives in it or for the bliddy tourists! And as for us scaring away ten thousand jobs, I'll tell yi this, boy! No civil servant will ever go without a job as long as good-for-nothing waster scum like us are still signing on at the DSS! Isn't that right, Jamesie?

JAMESIE. Here, here! Well done Rab, that needed to be said.

MAGISTRATE. That outburst will cost you dearly. You will each go to prison for ten days.

JAMESIE. (*To Nesbitt.*) I wisht you'd keep your gub shut once in a while. (*Shouts up.*) Ella doll! Will yi wait for me?

ELLA. Try and bliddy well stop me, *Aaron*!

JAMESIE. (*To policeman.*) Women, eh? (*No response.*) Aye, I know. I know. (*Skites himself.*) Shuttit you! (*Going.*) 'Mon, away we go . . .

They're led away.

SCENE 7. Glasgow. Day.
Montage of shots of Glasgow e.g. Princes Square, Georges Square, St Enoch Centre, City Chambers etc.

Glasgow 1990 theme tune.

SCENE 8. City Chambers function suite. Day.
Lord Provost, John and French dignitaries seated at dinner. Drink flowing. Provost and John a bit pissed.

PROVOST. (*With glass raised.*) Yi can't beat a good swally can yi, eh Pierre?

LEAD DIGNITARY. Pardon?

PROVOST. Le soup electrique! Chateau d'paralytica!

JOHN. Incidentally, Pierre. You see that picture above the Provost's head. That's a genuine Van Gogh, by the way!

LEAD DIGNITARY. Yes, I know. We loaned you it.

PROVOST. I should explain, Pierre. John here is the man we call Mr Glasgow. Anything you want to know about this city, John here's the boy to ask!

JOHN. (*Bashful.*) Ach . . .

PROVOST. Madelaine, hen! Would yi like to try him out? Go on, any question you like!

WOMAN DIGNITARY. No thank you.

LEAD DIGNITARY. (*Urging Dignitary 2.*) Madelaine . . .

JOHN. Her face has been tripping her all night. Are all communists as po-faced?

PROVOST. John . . . !

WOMAN DIGNITARY. Alright then, I'll ask a question about Glasgow.

PROVOST. That's the game, doll! Go ahead!

WOMAN DIGNITARY. Very well. What is the percentage of owner occupier in the class four sector of Govan? How many crimes are drink related? What is the incidence of rickets in . . .

JOHN. (*Indignant.*) Rickets? Are you trying to mix it, lady?

PROVOST. John, easy! You're embarrassing the company. (*To Dignitaries.*) Please excuse John. He's been under a strain recently. It's the artistic temperament, know.

LEAD DIGNITARY. John is an artist?

PROVOST. In a way, Pierre. He does a bit of creative accountancy, know. (*Winks.*) Yi know what a hassle it is, fiddling the old expensy-poos.

JOHN. Communists are all the same! (*To woman Dignitary.*) I suppose you think this city would be better run if we'd a socialist council?

PROVOST. John, we are a socialist council.

JOHN. I know that! I was being ironic! (*To woman Dignitary.*) Obviously the red carpet isnae good enough for you, lady!

WOMAN DIGNITARY. No it isn't. But it'll have to do, I suppose. Since it's the only red thing that's left on Clydeside.

PROVOST. (*Attempting to ease tension.*) Will yi listen to that, Pierre. The heady to and fro of intellectual discourse! I pure lap it up, don't you? Salut!

JOHN. (*Still fuming.*) You and yir bloody rickets, lady. I'll tell yi. Listen, you come along any time! Any time! We'll show you old punters, zombied with the finest tranquillisers! We'll show yi hospitals groaning with health care! Just oozing with it! Rickets!

DIGNITARY. Alright, I will.

JOHN. (*Slumps back in chair.*) Eh?

DIGNITARY. I'm a consultant neuro surgeon myself. But I'm always willing to learn. Will Friday do?

JOHN. (*At a loss.*) Well, er . . .

PROVOST. Certainmont, maddy! It'll be our treat! I'll just make the necessary arrangements, know? (*He laughs lightly, picks up a phone, begins stabbing out a number.*) (*To John, stabbing.*) See what you've started noo, ya tube? Now, I'll need to get that kidney machine out the lock-up and scour the dole for a coupla nurses.

JOHN. I said I'm sorry.

PROVOST. And while we're on the subject which end's neuro surgery. Is that the ass or the elbow?

Blank looks from both.

SCENE 9. Prison. Day.
Big sign. HM Prison Barlinnie. Nesbitt and Jamesie emerge from the prison, carrier bags full of belongings in hand. A prison officer shuts the door behind them.

NESBITT. (*To officer.*) Cheers pal, awrabest . . . Tell yi wan thing,

Cotter attempting to talk his wife Ella out of giving him a conjugal visit in prison.

Jamesie. See the jail? The jail's hardened me. From now on it's no more Mr Nice Guy!

JAMESIE. Me neither, Rab. See me, I'm a walking time bomb. I pity the man that messes with me.

A sudden shout.

MARY. Hey youse!

They jump, startled. Mary and Ella stand.

JAMESIE. (*Choked.*) Ella? Ella hen. I've missed yi more than words can say. (*Turning to go.*) See yi the night.

ELLA. (*Grabs him by the collar.*) Where'd yi think you're going, *Aaron*?

JAMESIE. Where'd yi think I'm going? I've done time behind bars. I need to do the simple things again. Sniff flooers! Feel the wind in my face! Reintegrate into Society!

ELLA. That's not what I asked yi. I says where are yi going?

JAMESIE. I'm away up the Two Ways to get blootered.

ELLA. Oh no you're not! You're going one way, pal. And that's right back hame to get your act cleaned up and some spondulix pamped in my purse.

JAMESIE. How am I going to do that, Ella?

ELLA. Why don't yi do a season at Ceaser's Palace, *Aaron*? (*Kicking.*) Move! Move!

JAMESIE. Aya! Watch it you. I'm a walking time bomb!

ELLA. Time warp more like. I says *move*.

She kicks his arse up the street. Nesbitt and Mary stand watching.

NESBITT. Tch! Wid yi look at that, Mary. In't is sad when two people can only communicate on the level of violence?

MARY. Aye. It is. (*She gives him a substantial skite across the chops with her message bag.*)

NESBITT. What was that for, by the way?

MARY. Don't talk to me you . . . ! (*Kicking.*) Ya good for nothing big . . .

SCENE 10. Street. Day.
*Same time. Gash and Burney across the street, watching Nesbitt and
Mary fighting.*

*Burney is down a drain. A battered pram full of rusty dangerous
looking objects close by.*

GASH. Look at that, eh? I love these traditional Glesga folk
dances, don't you?

BURNEY. Aye. Wonder what that yin is, eh.

GASH. Dunno. The dashing white scumball, maybes. (*Gives
Burney a gentle nudge with his boot.*) Anyway, never mind them!
'Mon you, back to work!

BURNEY. Aya! Gie's a Glesga work song well.

GASH. (*Singing, helping.*) I belang to the European City of
Culture . . .

BURNEY. (*Singing.*) Dear old European City of Culture toon . . .

SCENE 11. Street. Day.

*Nesbitt walking along the 'Art Shop' city street from Scene 4. He's
eating.*

NESBITT. (*To audience.*) Look at this, seen this? (*Shows.*) Pavarotti
chips – full of fat and pricey as hell. (*He stops by the tatty junk stall,
as before. Speaks to vendor.*) Awright pal? Yi happy at yir work?

VENDOR. Bugger aff.

NESBITT. (*To audience.*) That's Glesga for 'have a nice day.' (*To
vendor.*) Got any good keech in the day, pal? (*Picking a toy doll
up.*) What's this here?

VENDOR. That's the Glesga version of Tiny Tears. It's a dosser
doll. Gie it a squeeze and it puts its hon oot and begs ten pence
for a herbal tea.

He demonstrates.

NESBITT. (*To audience.*) I always said mechanisation would put
me oot of a job. (*To vendor.*) See you, boy. You want to be
ashamed of yourself. See people like you, you're exploiting
Glesga's heritage.

VENDOR. Why shouldn't I? What's my heritage ever done for me?

NESBITT. That's not the point. Coz I tell you this, boy – see me? See Glesga?

He's about to launch into a rant. Gash rushes up looking fraught.

GASH. Da, Da, come quick!

NESBITT. What's wrang? What's the matter?

GASH. It's Burney! He's kebabed himself with a railing. Get help! Pronto!

NESBITT. Where is he?

GASH. (*Points.*) There!

(*Burney, close by, in the pram. A rusty railing pokes out of his ankle.*)

BURNEY. 'Mon ya big swine, get your arse in gear and help.

NESBITT. (*To vendor.*) We'll resume this argument like civilised people later on! But see if I loss I'm gonny punch yir lights out, so be warned! (*To Gash.*) 'Mon you!

They rush off. The vendor picks up Nesbitt's abandoned chip poke from his stock. Grease runs everywhere. He registers distaste.

SCENE 12. City Street. Day.
Nesbitt pushing pram against a backdrop of architectural splendour, trying to hail a taxi.

NESBITT. (*Running, pushing pram, hailing.*) Haw, Jim! Haw, Jim!

The taxi stops up the street a bit.

NESBITT. Thank Christ for that!

Before Nesbitt gets to the taxi, two tourists get in. The taxi drives off as Nesbitt arrives up, panting.

NESBITT. Aye, don't bother with me! Just take the bliddy tourists. (*To Burney.*) Never you mind, son. Daddy's here.

BURNEY. Aye, that's magic. If it's all the same to you I'd sooner have a consultant surgeon! (*Strains to pull out the railing.*)

NESBITT. I'm trying, in't I! I'm trying!

Rab C. Nesbitt

Nesbitt hears a familiar voice from a short distance away.

JAMESIE. (*From offstage.*) Erzi year of sub culture! Ask me, genial Jamesie Cotter for details! Year of sub-culture!

Nesbitt looks. Jamesie stands on a box. A ring of tourists round him. He's pointing to a sign that says 'Glesga Year of Sub-culture', The two American tourists are there.

JAMESIE. (*Spieling.*) See the Glesga nobody knows! (*Showing items.*) Come with me now to a magic world of mutton pies, summonses and knocked off giro cheques!

WOMAN TOURIST. (*Indicating second sign.*) What's B & B & B?

JAMESIE. Bed, breakfast and Buckfast. (*Shows bottle.*) Here, Want to try it? Look why not, 'Live-in with authentic scum'. (*Indicates third sign.*)

WOMAN TOURIST. No, I don't think so.

JAMESIE. Ach, suit yirselves. But yeez don't know what yeez are missing.

MALE TOURIST. Scabies probably. (*Going.*) C'mon, Mo.

NESBITT. (*Calls.*) Hey, genial! It's not Buckfast that sign should say, it's fast buck! Why don't yi put on a grass skirt and be done with it?

GASH. Aye! You're nothing but an Uncle Tam!

NESBITT. (*Skitting Gash.*) Shuttit you! I'll do the social comment!

JAMESIE. (*Shouts back.*) Okay, so I'm a sell out! But I'll tell yi one thing. Thurs nothing like work for giving a man back his self respect. (*To a tourist. Sticking a scab to his face.*) There y'are boss! Tugging my forelock and pointing to my impetigo. Yi canny get more Glasgow than that, can yi? (*The tourist takes a picture, his wife gives Jamesie a coin.*) (*Ingratiating.*) Thanks very much, madam (*Kissing hand.*) Haste yi back. God bless America!!

Nesbitt, Gash and Burney – Nesbitt fuming. Gash throwing up.

NESBITT. Ya durty wee sookmatorrie yi! I'll tell you one thing boy! See me? See Glesga . . . ?

BURNEY. (*Interjecting.*) Haw Da! I don't want you thinking I'm a hypochondriac nor nothing. But we'll need to get up that hospital fast.

NESBITT. How son?

BURNEY. (*Holding it up.*) My foot's just dropped off.

NESBITT. (*Grips pram, swaying.*) In the namea ... (*Shouts to Jamesie.*) I'll deal with you later, Rastus. 'Mon boys ...!

They hurry off.

SCENE 13. Reception area of a hospital. Day.

Doors burst open. Nesbitt enters pushing pram. We track him as he goes. People scatter.

NESBITT. (*To receptionist, as he goes.*) Hey doll! My boy's been malkied. Is that the chib unit.

RECEPTIONIST. It's casualty, yes. But you can't go there! The Lord Provost's in there.

NESBITT. It's awright, I've had swine fever. 'Mon Gash.

He storms on.

SCENE 14. Casualty ward. Day.
Nurse in background, tidying a bed.

Provost, John, the two Dignitaries around an old woman who's lying ill in bed.

PROVOST. As you can see, Pierre, in the new Glasgow, compassion is our watchword. No expense is spared to ease the sufferings of the infirm. (*Moving old woman's head, roughly.*) Shift you, and let Pierre feel that duckdown pillow. Allez! Vite!

Lead Dignitary feels the pillow, tentatively.

JOHN. The Provost's right, Pierre. The way we see it, people might be diseased, but they can still have eye appeal. Look. (*Whips back old woman's covers to reveal.*) Charles Rennie McIntosh rubber sheet. Go on run your hand over that moquette effect.

LEAD DIGNITARY. (*Doubtfully.*) I don't think so.

PROVOST. (*To woman Dignitary.*) And look, Madeleine.

Something for the ladies. A kidney machine in spleen pink. Ambiance is so important, even in a charnel house, don't you think?

WOMAN DIGNITARY. Yes. But tell me. (*Picking up lead.*) Why is there no plug on it?

JOHN. (*Snatching lead.*) Gimmee that! Trust you to pick faults!

PROVOST. (*To lead Dignitary, handing out drinks.*) So you see, Pierre, the bad old image of Glasgow is gone forever. If indeed it ever existed.

JOHN. Exactly! And as the city fathers, we're proud to take our rightful place among the great cultural centres of the world. Just ahead of Florence.

PROVOST. And slightly behind Blackpool. (*Raising glass*) Cheers!

ALL. (*Raising glasses.*) Cheers!

Doors burst open. Nesbitt enters, pushing pram, followed by Gash. Burney is unconscious.

NESBITT. (*Clocking them.*) Hey, ya drunken bams! Is this what I dodged my poll tax for?

PROVOST. (*To John.*) In the namea . . . , John! Bigfoot's back!

NESBITT. Aye. And I've brung my litter with me! Meet wee foot! (*Chucks Burney's foot at him.*) Catch!

PROVOST. (*Horrified.*) In the namea . . . That's ghastly!

JOHN. Aye. And in a Woolies trainer.

A doctor appears. The receptionist enters behind Nesbitt.

DOCTOR. I'm Doctor McOrton! What the hell's going on here?

RECEPTIONIST. I'm sorry, doctor, I tried to stop him! But you know the strength of these people!

PROVOST. (*To doctor.*) Would you take this? It's in need of a major pedicure.

WOMAN DIGNITARY. (*Looking at foot.*) Doctor, this limb could be saved. Is there a micro surgeon in the building?

DOCTOR. No.

WOMAN DIGNITARY. In that case I will perform the operation myself.

DOCTOR. You?

LEAD DIGNITARY. Doctor, Madelaine is a lecturer in micro surgery at the L'ecole de Medicine in Paris. She is fully competent.

DOCTOR. I don't know. This is most unusual. I'd have to ask permission of the parent.

NESBITT. (*To woman Dignitary.*) Doll, you fix my wee action man here and my porte will always be ouvried to you! And yi don't even need to bring a carry oot, there y'are!

WOMAN DIGNITARY. In that case there is no time to lose. Doctor?

DOCTOR. (*Swaddling foot in towel.*) Let's go . . . !

They go.

NESBITT. (*Shouts.*) Haw! Are yeez not forgetting something?

Lead Dignitary and Doctor freeze.

DOCTOR. What?

NESBITT. (*Propels pram towards them.*) The rest of him.

Sheepish looks as they hurry away, pushing pram.

SCENE 15. The Nesbitt's house. Day.
A French tricolour flutters from an improvised mast, outside the Nesbitt's house. Quick blast of the Marseillaise.

Mary sitting on a chair on the pavement, outside the house, knitting.

MARY. (*To audience.*) I take it yeez saw it? Rab's concession to European culture. Other hooses get a satellite dish, we get a clothes pole with a table cloth stuck to it. Ach, but I don't blame him. And at least we've got more international brotherhood than some people I could name.

A little way down the street. Ella and Jamesie appear. She kicking Jamesie up the behind as they walk.

ELLA. (*Kicking.*) Ya useless bliddy article! You're not a man, you're neuter!

173

JAMESIE. Aya! It wasnie my fault, Ella! It was my punters. I educated them out of their class!

MARY. (*As they draw level.*) What the hell's the matter with youse pair?

ELLA. Don't ask me, ask Jungle Jamesie here, he'll tell yi!

JAMESIE. Honest to God, Mary. All's I did was run a few tourists about, to show them the local folk art, know? The simple joys of pummelling the Provident man, sticking a magnet to the electric meter, and following the postman to knock giros out his haversack.

MARY. Sounds reasonable to me.

ELLA. Aye! Now tell her what happened while yi were doing it!

JAMESIE. Would yi believe it, Mary. But some durty thieving bamstick broke in and stole wur video!

MARY. Tch! And I can mind the days when yi could leave your door wide open tae.

ELLA. I ask yi, Mary. What kinna mind would do a thing like that?

MARY. Obviously a diseased mind, Ella. A disgrace to this fair city of ours!

SCENE 16. The Nesbitts' living room. Day.
Close up on a big toe stretching through the hole in a sock to operate the rewind button on a video recorder.

NESBITT. (*From offstage, singing.*) 'Naw, nae regrets. Naw there will be nae regrets . . . ' (*To audience.*) Tell yi wan thing, see the Europeans? Some sense of humour, by the way. How they can make Glesga City of Culture and still keep a straight face, it's some going. Coz see keech like me, we're getting a hard time offa the shortbread set just coz it's 1990. (*Mimicking a Kelvinside [a very smart part of Glasgow] accent*) 'Stereotypes like him give Glasgow a bad name. We want Van Gogh.' And the best of it is, Van Gogh was a worse heidbanger than I am too! If I met Van Gogh in the lavvy of the Two Ways I'd do a U-turn in case he chibbed me with a palette knife. And what did he ever paint anyhow? I'll tell yi, it's just as well Van Gogh wasnie from Kelvinside or he widnae have painted nothing! (*In a Kelvinside accent*) 'Oh there's a dod of scum picking totties in the field but I better not paint him. He's a cultural stereotype.' Get tae . . . ! Do I sound angry by the way? I bliddy well hope so! Coz making yir own blood boil is the only way yi can keep warm in the city, there y'are! So don't culture me, boy! Yi canny get a bus on a Sunday night, but I'm supposed to be up to high doh coz Pavarotti's gonny tickle his tonsils! Get tae . . . ! (*He stabs a button on the television remote control panel.*) Bliddy culture . . . !

TELLY VOICE. And now, the highlight of the year's cultural celebrations. Luciano Pavarotti, live from Glasgow.

NESBITT. Well yi might be live in Glesga, boy! But yir bloody well deid in Govan! Take one step up my street and I'll stick my boot right up yir arias! (*Railing at telly.*) I don't want your culture! You can keep yir culture! I don't bliddy well want it! (*He picks up the telly.*)

SCENE 17. Nesbitts' house. Day.
Mary and Jamesie as before.

JAMESIE. I'll tell yi wan thing, Mary. It's at times of crisis like these I draw strength from my heritage. Remember that good old Glesga saying. No matter how bad things are, there's always somebody worse off than yirself. Adios!

They share a smile. He walks a couple of steps.

The Nesbitt window.

NESBITT. (*From offstage shouts.*) Keep yir bliddy culture!

The telly comes crashing in a wide arc through the window.

The telly clunks Jamesie on the side of the head.

JAMESIE. (*Dazed.*) In the namea . . .

He staggers a couple more steps, drops, suddenly, out of sight down an open drain with a startled yell.

Same time, same place. Burney standing, on crutches, over the open drain. His foot's back on.

BURNEY. (*To audience*) God bless us, one and all.

JAMESIE. (*From offstage down drain.*) Burney son! Get yir Da! Hurry up! (*Groans.*)

BURNEY. (*To audience.*) Well, most of us, anyhow. Stupid bam.

He slides the drain cover into place with his plastered foot. It clunks, satisfyingly, into position.

BURNEY. (*Hailing.*) Haw! Taxi!

Gash pulls up in a pram wheeled 'bogie'. Burney gets on.

JAMESIE. (*Down drain.*) Haw! Naw! Wait a minute! Haw, boys! Boys!

Gash and Burney coasting down the street in the bogie. They're singing . . . 'I belang to the European City of Culture. Dear old . . . '